JAWAHARLAL NEHRU

WORLD LEADERS PAST & PRESENT

JAWAHARLAL NEHRU

Lila Finck and John P. Hayes

1987
CHELSEA HOUSE PUBLISHERS
NEW YORK
NEW HAVEN PHILADELPHIA

EDITORIAL DIRECTOR: Nancy Toff
MANAGING EDITOR: Karyn Gullen Browne
COPY CHIEF: Perry Scott King
ART DIRECTOR: Giannella Garrett
ASSISTANT ART DIRECTOR: Carol McDougall
PICTURE EDITOR: Elizabeth Terhune

Staff for JAWAHARLAL NEHRU:

SENIOR EDITOR: John W. Selfridge
ASSISTANT EDITORS: Maria Behan, Pierre Hauser, Howard Ratner, Bert Yaeger
COPY EDITORS: Sean Dolan, Kathleen McDermott
ASSISTANT DESIGNER: Noreen Lamb
PICTURE RESEARCH: Diane Wallis
LAYOUT: Irene Friedman
PRODUCTION COORDINATOR: Alma Rodriguez
PRODUCTION ASSISTANT: Karen Dreste
COVER ILLUSTRATION: Michael Garland

CREATIVE DIRECTOR: Harold Steinberg

Frontispiece courtesy of AP/Wide World Photos

First Printing

Library of Congress Cataloging in Publication Data

Finck, Lila. JAWAHARLAL NEHRU

(World leaders past & present)
Bibliography: p.
Includes index.
1. Nehru, Jawaharlal, 1889–1964—Juvenile literature.
2. Prime ministers—India—Biography—Juvenile literature.
[1. Nehru, Jawaharlal, 1889–1964. 2. Prime ministers]
I. Hayes, John Phillip, 1949–
II. Title. III. Series.
DS481.N35F56   1987   954.04'2'0924 [B] [92]   86-24488

ISBN 0-87754-543-X

Contents

CHELSEA HOUSE PUBLISHERS

WORLD LEADERS PAST & PRESENT

ADENAUER
ALEXANDER THE GREAT
MARC ANTONY
KING ARTHUR
ATATÜRK
ATTLEE
BEGIN
BEN-GURION
BISMARCK
LÉON BLUM
BOLÍVAR
CESARE BORGIA
BRANDT
BREZHNEV
CAESAR
CALVIN
CASTRO
CATHERINE THE GREAT
CHARLEMAGNE
CHIANG KAI-SHEK
CHURCHILL
CLEMENCEAU
CLEOPATRA
CORTÉS
CROMWELL
DANTON
DE GAULLE
DE VALERA
DISRAELI
EISENHOWER
ELEANOR OF AQUITAINE
QUEEN ELIZABETH I
FERDINAND AND ISABELLA
FRANCO

FREDERICK THE GREAT
INDIRA GANDHI
MOHANDAS GANDHI
GARIBALDI
GENGHIS KHAN
GLADSTONE
GORBACHEV
HAMMARSKJÖLD
HENRY VIII
HENRY OF NAVARRE
HINDENBURG
HITLER
HO CHI MINH
HUSSEIN
IVAN THE TERRIBLE
ANDREW JACKSON
JEFFERSON
JOAN OF ARC
POPE JOHN XXIII
LYNDON JOHNSON
JUÁREZ
JOHN F. KENNEDY
KENYATTA
KHOMEINI
KHRUSHCHEV
MARTIN LUTHER KING, JR.
KISSINGER
LENIN
LINCOLN
LLOYD GEORGE
LOUIS XIV
LUTHER
JUDAS MACCABEUS
MAO ZEDONG

MARY, QUEEN OF SCOTS
GOLDA MEIR
METTERNICH
MUSSOLINI
NAPOLEON
NASSER
NEHRU
NERO
NICHOLAS II
NIXON
NKRUMAH
PERICLES
PERÓN
QADDAFI
ROBESPIERRE
ELEANOR ROOSEVELT
FRANKLIN D. ROOSEVELT
THEODORE ROOSEVELT
SADAT
STALIN
SUN YAT-SEN
TAMERLANE
THATCHER
TITO
TROTSKY
TRUDEAU
TRUMAN
VICTORIA
WASHINGTON
WEIZMANN
WOODROW WILSON
XERXES
ZHOU ENLAI

ON LEADERSHIP
Arthur M. Schlesinger, jr.

LEADERSHIP, it may be said, is really what makes the world go round. Love no doubt smooths the passage; but love is a private transaction between consenting adults. Leadership is a public transaction with history. The idea of leadership affirms the capacity of individuals to move, inspire, and mobilize masses of people so that they act together in pursuit of an end. Sometimes leadership serves good purposes, sometimes bad; but whether the end is benign or evil, great leaders are those men and women who leave their personal stamp on history.

Now, the very concept of leadership implies the proposition that individuals can make a difference. This proposition has never been universally accepted. From classical times to the present day, eminent thinkers have regarded individuals as no more than the agents and pawns of larger forces, whether the gods and goddesses of the ancient world or, in the modern era, race, class, nation, the dialectic, the will of the people, the spirit of the times, history itself. Against such forces, the individual dwindles into insignificance.

So contends the thesis of historical determinism. Tolstoy's great novel *War and Peace* offers a famous statement of the case. Why, Tolstoy asked, did millions of men in the Napoleonic wars, denying their human feelings and their common sense, move back and forth across Europe slaughtering their fellows? "The war," Tolstoy answered, "was bound to happen simply because it was bound to happen." All prior history predetermined it. As for leaders, they, Tolstoy said, "are but the labels that serve to give a name to an end and, like labels, they have the least possible connection with the event." The greater the leader, "the more conspicuous the inevitability and the predestination of every act he commits." The leader, said Tolstoy, is "the slave of history."

Determinism takes many forms. Marxism is the determinism of class. Nazism the determinism of race. But the idea of men and women as the slaves of history runs athwart the deepest human instincts. Rigid determinism abolishes the idea of human freedom—

the assumption of free choice that underlies every move we make, every word we speak, every thought we think. It abolishes the idea of human responsibility, since it is manifestly unfair to reward or punish people for actions that are by definition beyond their control. No one can live consistently by any deterministic creed. The Marxist states prove this themselves by their extreme susceptibility to the cult of leadership.

More than that, history refutes the idea that individuals make no difference. In December 1931 a British politician crossing Park Avenue in New York City between 76th and 77th Streets around 10:30 P.M. looked in the wrong direction and was knocked down by an automobile—a moment, he later recalled, of a man aghast, a world aglare: "I do not understand why I was not broken like an eggshell or squashed like a gooseberry." Fourteen months later an American politician, sitting in an open car in Miami, Florida, was fired on by an assassin; the man beside him was hit. Those who believe that individuals make no difference to history might well ponder whether the next two decades would have been the same had Mario Constasino's car killed Winston Churchill in 1931 and Giuseppe Zangara's bullet killed Franklin Roosevelt in 1933. Suppose, in addition, that Adolf Hitler had been killed in the street fighting during the Munich *Putsch* of 1923 and that Lenin had died of typhus during World War I. What would the 20th century be like now?

For better or for worse, individuals do make a difference. "The notion that a people can run itself and its affairs anonymously," wrote the philosopher William James, "is now well known to be the silliest of absurdities. Mankind does nothing save through initiatives on the part of inventors, great or small, and imitation by the rest of us—these are the sole factors in human progress. Individuals of genius show the way, and set the patterns, which common people then adopt and follow."

Leadership, James suggests, means leadership in thought as well as in action. In the long run, leaders in thought may well make the greater difference to the world. But, as Woodrow Wilson once said, "Those only are leaders of men, in the general eye, who lead in action. . . . It is at their hands that new thought gets its translation into the crude language of deeds." Leaders in thought often invent in solitude and obscurity, leaving to later generations the tasks of imitation. Leaders in action—the leaders portrayed in this series—have to be effective in their own time.

And they cannot be effective by themselves. They must act in response to the rhythms of their age. Their genius must be adapted, in a phrase of William James's, "to the receptivities of the moment." Leaders are useless without followers. "There goes the mob," said the French politician hearing a clamor in the streets. "I am their leader. I must follow them." Great leaders turn the inchoate emotions of the mob to purposes of their own. They seize on the opportunities of their time, the hopes, fears, frustrations, crises, potentialities. They succeed when events have prepared the way for them, when the community is awaiting to be aroused, when they can provide the clarifying and organizing ideas. Leadership ignites the circuit between the individual and the mass and thereby alters history.

It may alter history for better or for worse. Leaders have been responsible for the most extravagant follies and most monstrous crimes that have beset suffering humanity. They have also been vital in such gains as humanity has made in individual freedom, religious and racial tolerance, social justice and respect for human rights.

There is no sure way to tell in advance who is going to lead for good and who for evil. But a glance at the gallery of men and women in *World Leaders—Past and Present* suggests some useful tests.

One test is this: do leaders lead by force or by persuasion? By command or by consent? Through most of history leadership was exercised by the divine right of authority. The duty of followers was to defer and to obey. "Theirs not to reason why,/ Theirs but to do and die." On occasion, as with the so-called "enlightened despots" of the 18th century in Europe, absolutist leadership was animated by humane purposes. More often, absolutism nourished the passion for domination, land, gold and conquest and resulted in tyranny.

The great revolution of modern times has been the revolution of equality. The idea that all people should be equal in their legal condition has undermined the old structure of authority, hierarchy and deference. The revolution of equality has had two contrary effects on the nature of leadership. For equality, as Alexis de Tocqueville pointed out in his great study *Democracy in America,* might mean equality in servitude as well as equality in freedom.

"I know of only two methods of establishing equality in the political world," Tocqueville wrote. "Rights must be given to every citizen, or none at all to anyone . . . save one, who is the master of all." There was no middle ground "between the sovereignty of all and the absolute power of one man." In his astonishing prediction of 20th-century totalitarian dictatorship, Tocqueville explained how the revolution of equality could lead to the *"Führerprinzip"* and more terrible absolutism than the world had ever known.

But when rights are given to every citizen and the sovereignty of all is established, the problem of leadership takes a new form, becomes more exacting than ever before. It is easy to issue commands and enforce them by the rope and the stake, the concentration camp and the *gulag.* It is much harder to use argument and achievement to overcome opposition and win consent. The Founding Fathers of the United States understood the difficulty. They believed that history had given them the opportunity to decide, as Alexander Hamilton wrote in the first Federalist Paper, whether men are indeed capable of basing government on "reflection and choice, or whether they are forever destined to depend . . . on accident and force."

Government by reflection and choice called for a new style of leadership and a new quality of followership. It required leaders to be responsive to popular concerns, and it required followers to be active and informed participants in the process. Democracy does not eliminate emotion from politics; sometimes it fosters demagoguery; but it is confident that, as the greatest of democratic leaders put it, you cannot fool all of the people all of the time. It measures leadership by results and retires those who overreach or falter or fail.

It is true that in the long run despots are measured by results too. But they can postpone the day of judgment, sometimes indefinitely, and in the meantime they can do infinite harm. It is also true that democracy is no guarantee of virtue and intelligence in government, for the voice of the people is not necessarily the voice of God. But democracy, by assuring the right of opposition, offers built-in resistance to the evils inherent in absolutism. As the theologian Reinhold Niebuhr summed it up, "Man's capacity for justice makes democracy possible, but man's inclination to injustice makes democracy necessary."

A second test for leadership is the end for which power is sought. When leaders have as their goal the supremacy of a master race or the promotion of totalitarian revolution or the acquisition and exploitation of colonies or the protection of greed and privilege or the preservation of personal power, it is likely that their leadership will do little to advance the cause of humanity. When their goal is the abolition of slavery, the liberation of women, the enlargement of opportunity for the poor and powerless, the extension of equal rights to racial minorities, the defense of the freedoms of expression and opposition, it is likely that their leadership will increase the sum of human liberty and welfare.

Leaders have done great harm to the world. They have also conferred great benefits. You will find both sorts in this series. Even "good" leaders must be regarded with a certain wariness. Leaders are not demigods; they put on their trousers one leg after another just like ordinary mortals. No leader is infallible, and every leader needs to be reminded of this at regular intervals. Irreverence irritates leaders but is their salvation. Unquestioning submission corrupts leaders and demands followers. Making a cult of a leader is always a mistake. Fortunately hero worship generates its own antidote. "Every hero," said Emerson, "becomes a bore at last."

The signal benefit the great leaders confer is to embolden the rest of us to live according to our own best selves, to be active, insistent, and resolute in affirming our own sense of things. For great leaders attest to the reality of human freedom against the supposed inevitabilities of history. And they attest to the wisdom and power that may lie within the most unlikely of us, which is why Abraham Lincoln remains the supreme example of great leadership. A great leader, said Emerson, exhibits new possibilities to all humanity. "We feed on genius. . . . Great men exist that there may be greater men."

Great leaders, in short, justify themselves by emancipating and empowering their followers. So humanity struggles to master its destiny, remembering with Alexis de Tocqueville: "It is true that around every man a fatal circle is traced beyond which he cannot pass; but within the wide verge of that circle he is powerful and free; as it is with man, so with communities."

—*New York*

1

The Early Years

A huge crowd gathered in the holy city of Amritsar on April 13, 1919, for the Hindu New Year's Day. Peasant men, women, and children from neighboring villages met in the beautiful garden of Jallianwalla Bagh. The people gathered to hear speeches protesting unfair treatment of Indians by the British authorities.

Indian resentment of the British, who had been India's colonial rulers since the late 1700s, had been building for a long time. In 1857 there had been a widespread revolt against the British East India Company, which had maintained a monopoly on all trade in the area for almost a century. Indian forces, led by princes and rulers of different Indian states and provinces, tried to regain the kingdoms they had previously lost to the British East India Company. All of India's major religious groups — Hindus, Muslims, and Sikhs — joined in the fight. But the British put down the rebellion and defeated the Indians. One year later India's government was taken over by the British crown, and the country formally became part of the British Empire.

After the British took power, many well-to-do In-

I would say that democracy is not only political, not only economic, but something of the mind, as is everything. It involves equality of opportunity for all people. It involves the freedom of the individual to grow and to make the best of his capacity and ability. It involves a certain tolerance of others and even of others' opinions when they differ from yours.
—JAWAHARLAL NEHRU

Jawaharlal Nehru, at age eight, and his mother, Swaruprani, in 1897. Nehru was born into a wealthy family of the Brahman caste — India's highest social class. As a privileged child, he had many private tutors and quickly developed a love for science and English poetry.

Mohandas K. Gandhi, also known as the Mahatma, or Great Soul. Gandhi is considered the architect of Indian independence. His nonviolent campaign of civil disobedience to end British rule in India made him one of the towering political and spiritual figures of the 20th century.

dian families migrated to big cities expecting to find business opportunities and a chance to work for the new British government. By cooperating with local officials, they hoped to improve British-Indian relations. They also hoped to eventually establish a more democratic form of government.

In 1885, with British approval, a group of educated Indians met in Bombay and organized the Indian National Congress. The Congress did not have an established meeting place but met at certain times in different locations to discuss India's problems and to involve more Indians in the local government. Members of the Indian National Congress included representatives from various Indian states and provinces and members of the different religious groups.

The majority of these representatives were not strong nationalists. They did not believe that India's government should be completely separated from the British government. They were against protest demonstrations that might lead to violence. But a few congressmen started listening to a man who talked about new, peaceful ways of protesting against British rule. His name was Mohandas Karamchand Gandhi.

Relations between Britain and India continued to deteriorate. When Gandhi introduced his new way of attacking the problem of colonial rule, these relations reached a critical point. Gandhi's idea was to resist oppression by methods of peaceful resistance. This was his philosophy of *satyagraha*. His followers were known as *satyagrahi*.

Marchers wearing homespun garments accompany a giant symbolic spinning wheel in a 1922 procession led by Gandhi. The Mahatma believed that native methods of manufacturing, using traditional techniques such as the spinning wheel, were the best way for the country to achieve economic regeneration on its own terms.

British soldiers attack *satyagrahi* (followers of Gandhi's protest methods) in 1930; the Indians refused to strike back and suffered nearly 500 casualties. After the notorious British massacre of nearly 400 unarmed Indians at Amritsar on April 13, 1919, Nehru had finally realized the injustice and immorality of the British presence in India.

> *I fired and continued to fire until the crowd dispersed, and I considered this the least amount of firing which would produce the necessary moral and widespread effect it was my duty to produce. If more troops had been at hand, the casualties would have been in greater proportion.*
> —GENERAL R. E. H. DYER
> British commander at the Jallianwalla Bagh massacre

By 1919 many of India's poor and oppressed had become followers of Gandhi. He taught people non-violent ways to protest against unfair treatment by their enemies. Gandhi believed in prayer and peaceful resistance to the British oppression.

In recent years, British dominance had become intolerably repressive. The people of India were losing their rights. Soon they were denied the rights to free speech and to a fair trial. An independence movement was now well established under the leadership of Gandhi.

It was unlawful for the New Year's crowd to gather at Jallianwalla Bagh, although most of the peasants didn't know it. A few days before, Brigadier General Reginald Dyer, the British official in charge of Amritsar, had declared martial law in the city. This law banned all public meetings and gatherings because they might lead to a riot. General Dyer ordered his men to post warning notices on public buildings and hand out leaflets about the law. But many peasants could not read, and most of those who could did not understand the law. The people arrived to celebrate the holiday without concern.

However, when General Dyer heard about the

rally, this tough disciplinarian decided to teach the Indians a lesson. He would punish the troublemakers. He accompanied 50 armed soldiers to the entrance of the public garden. They arrived in the middle of a speech by a village leader. The soldiers ordered the crowd to disperse, but there was no escape. High walls enclosed the park on three sides. Several houses formed the fourth boundary. The soldiers blocked the only exit.

Suddenly, General Dyer ordered the soldiers to fire. A hail of bullets at point-blank range exploded into the unarmed crowd. Desperately, people ran in all directions. Many tried to protect their frightened children. Some attempted to climb the walls to safety, only to be cut down by bullets. The soldiers continued shooting for 10 minutes, until all their ammunition was gone. As they filed out of the gardens, they left behind one of India's bloodiest massacres.

Jawaharlal Nehru, an assistant attorney in the court at Amritsar, was among the members of the Indian National Congress who investigated the tragedy. Nearly 400 Indian peasants were killed and almost 1,200 were wounded by British soldiers that day. Nehru was sickened by the bloodshed, but, most of all, he was horrified by General Dyer's vicious brutality at Amritsar. "I realized then, more vividly than I had ever done before, how brutal and immoral imperialism was and how it had eaten into the souls of the British upper classes," he said. This terrible event was an important turning point for Nehru. Almost 30 years later he would become the first prime minister of an independent India.

On November 14, 1889, the day Nehru was born, there was great rejoicing in the Nehru household. Poor people gathered near the Nehru home and received food as part of the celebration. Jawaharlal (which means "Precious Jewel") was much loved and cherished by his parents.

The Nehrus were a wealthy family from Kashmir, India's northernmost state, located in the Himalayan mountains. Motilal Nehru and his wife, Swaruprani, were members of the highest Hindu social

> *In my humble opinion, non-cooperation with evil is as much a duty as is cooperation with good.*
> —MOHANDAS K. GANDHI
> Hindu nationalist leader

17

class, or caste, called *Brahmans*. Motilal Nehru was a successful lawyer who arrived in the city of Allahabad in 1886. Within a short time, besides becoming one of the most outstanding lawyers in Allahabad, Motilal became an important member of the Indian National Congress when it met there the year before Jawaharlal was born. Meeting there despite British disapproval was a test of the Indians' will and determination.

Allahabad, then capital of India's North-West Provinces, was also the city in which the British lieutenant governor, Sir Auckland Colvin, was based. He argued against allowing the Indians their own representative assembly. Democracy, he claimed, could not work in a society where tensions existed between two major religious groups — the Hindus and the Muslims.

When Jawaharlal was almost 10, his family moved into an elegant Victorian mansion in an upper-class, residential part of Allahabad. They named the mansion *Anand Bhawan*, which means "Abode of Happiness." The house was surrounded by extensive gardens, verandas, and beautifully landscaped terraces. There was a stable for the family horses. There was also a tennis court and swimming pool, which was quite unusual in Allahabad. Ordinarily, only the local members of the British aristocracy lived in such grand style.

The Nehrus entertained many famous people at Anand Bhawan. As a little boy, Nehru enjoyed peeking from behind the curtains to see the famous guests who visited his father, but he was afraid that if he was discovered, he might be spanked. Motilal had an explosive temper that everyone in the family feared.

During his childhood, Nehru received his education at home. He had private tutors and governesses. One of his favorite tutors was a young Irishman named Ferdinand Brooks, who taught him to read and to love English literature and poetry. But the subject he did best in was science. Brooks set up a small laboratory for Nehru, and together the tutor and the young student conducted scientific experiments that Nehru greatly enjoyed.

Motilal Nehru, Jawaharlal's father, in 1930. Motilal was a prosperous lawyer who at first expected his son to practice law in the British-controlled courts, but later himself joined the independence movement. Nehru cited Motilal and Gandhi as the two supreme influences in his life.

When he was 15, Nehru traveled to England in order to enroll in Harrow, a private school for wealthy boys. At Harrow, he was away from the protection and loving security of his family for the first time. The separation was difficult for him and equally difficult for his father. After Motilal left Jawaharlal at school, he wrote him a letter expressing how he felt: "In you we are leaving the dearest treasure we have in this world and perhaps in worlds to come. . . . It would be sinful to keep you with us

Nehru and his sister Sarup in 1903. Under her married name, Vijaya Laksmi Pandit, she played an active role in the struggle for India's independence. Later, as leader of her country's delegation to the United Nations from 1946 to 1948, she became the first woman president of the General Assembly.

and leave you a fortune in gold with little or no education. . . . I never thought I loved you as much as when I had to part from you."

Jawaharlal was a quiet, serious student at Harrow. He passed his examinations with high honors. His academic abilities did little to help the homesickness and loneliness he felt. Although he played team sports such as cricket and rowing at school, he regarded himself a loner. He thought that he did not fit in with the others. Although he found friends who were English, he knew at this early age that he could not be the friend of the British government.

During Nehru's two years at Harrow, he kept informed about events at home. Even before 1912, when he returned to India, the idea of nationalism appealed to Nehru. He wanted to join the nationalists. He believed in Indian independence and was willing to fight for it. Under their leader Bal Gangadhar Tilak, the nationalists — those who wanted complete independence for India — earnestly campaigned for Indian independence, eventually forming the Home Rule League in April 1916. Tilak was voted out of the Indian National Congress and called a "radical extremist" by the conservative members of Congress, including Motilal.

Motilal wrote to Jawaharlal and told him not to get involved with nationalist extremists. He advised his son to remain loyal to the British Empire. Motilal wanted Jawaharlal to follow in his footsteps — to study law in England and afterward practice his profession in Allahabad.

Jawaharlal was disappointed by his father's attitude. He thought students should get involved in politics. And although he respected his father,

Women members of the Nationalist party at their convention in Bombay in 1922. Women participated with equal fervor in Gandhi's efforts to remake the Indian consciousness.

Nehru was not sure he wanted to be a lawyer.

Before he was 18, Nehru completed his studies at Harrow and entered Trinity College at Cambridge University in England. He was now a slim, handsome young man who spoke with a distinct English accent. Not only did Nehru have a firm command of European history and literature, he was also interested in British politics. Nehru was attracted to the extreme political movements he found close at hand, especially the nationalists in Ireland, known as Sinn Fein.

After Cambridge, he followed his father's wishes and went to London to study law at the Inner Temple. London was full of excitement for young Nehru. He ate in all the best restaurants, wore fashionably tailored clothes, and generally lived the life of a wealthy British gentleman. He spent a lot of money, and Motilal, who paid the bills, was concerned that his son was neither a serious student nor a devout believer in Hindu custom. He wrote to Jawaharlal and told him that he would forgive him for living so extravagantly if he promised to marry a Hindu Kashmiri girl when he returned to India.

In fact, while Jawaharlal was in England, his parents had been searching for a wife for him. Young Indians were expected to marry someone chosen for them by their families — a tradition Jawaharlal thought was old-fashioned.

One day Jawaharlal received a photograph of a young girl his father hoped he would marry. He immediately wrote home, "There is not an atom of romance in the way you are searching girls for me and keeping them waiting till my arrival. The very idea is extremely unromantic. . . . The girl whose photograph you sent me is probably a nice person, but I can hardly say I am enamoured of her from the photo." Jawaharlal, however, did agree to marry her upon his return to India.

Although he had not studied very seriously during the time he was in London, Nehru received his law degree and was licensed to practice law in 1912. His formal education in England was complete. He was 23 years old when he left England and returned to his homeland.

Followers of Gandhi continue their spinning while in prison in 1921. India's independence leaders were frequently jailed for their beliefs — Gandhi for a total of over six years, and Nehru for nine years. Both chose to accept the legal consequences of civil disobedience and refused to use violence.

2

A New Awakening

When Nehru returned to Allahabad in 1912, he found that life at home had changed little. Several nationalist extremists had been jailed. The Indian National Congress was still loyal to Britain. Within Nehru's own family, his sister Sarup was almost 12. Another sister, Krishna, had been born while Nehru was away at school. Motilal's influential friends and associates were still meeting at Anand Bhawan to talk about politics and legal matters.

Meanwhile, Gandhi's peaceful protest tactics had been tried out with success in India in 1916 at a place called Champaran, on the edge of the Himalayas, a few hundred miles from Allahabad. Nehru's political idealism was excited by this humble figure who seemed to Nehru "clear-cut and hard as a diamond." Nehru wanted desperately to join the satyagraha movement. His father, on the other hand, had been steeped in the law; he found civil disobedience, at first, to be unacceptable in the attempt to gain more freedom for the Indian people. Motilal's son first glimpsed Gandhi in 1915 when the white-robed man with eyeglasses attended the Congress in Bombay. In 1916 Nehru met the leader, who,

India must conquer her so-called conquerors by love. For us, patriotism is the same as the love of humanity.
—MOHANDAS K. GANDHI

Nehru as a member of England's Cambridge University training corps in 1910. The political debates in England at the time focused on socialism, Irish Home Rule, and women's suffrage, all of which contributed to the ideas Nehru brought back to India.

The Nehru family, circa 1910. Counterclockwise from Jawaharlal, who is seated in the center: Swaruprani, his mother; an English governess; Brijlal, a cousin; Motilal, Jawaharlal's father; Brijlal's wife; and Mrs. Zutshi, another cousin.

while a young lawyer, helped Indians fight against discrimination in South Africa during the late 19th and early 20th centuries. The differences of opinion between Motilal and his son finally became so intense that he asked Gandhi himself to talk with the younger Nehru. Nehru was told by his idol not to act against his father's wishes. But even this did not prevent events — and Nehru's nationalist fervor —from pressuring Motilal.

Nehru tried to settle down and work with his father as an assistant lawyer, but he soon became bored. He found the courtroom monotonous. More interesting to him was the All-India Home Rule League, a nationalist organization that campaigned for Indian independence, broadening the efforts of Tilak's Home Rule League. The All-India Home Rule League was led by Annie Besant, an old family friend.

Besant was an energetic and persuasive woman who had left Ireland, her homeland, to live in India. She strongly favored Indian freedom and was a well-known nationalist. Sixty-nine-year-old Besant urged all Indians to join local branches of the Home Rule movement and fight for Indian independence.

In 1916 Annie Besant toured the country and made rousing speeches about India's future as a free nation. She argued that if Indian soldiers were expected to fight in World War I — the bloody conflict that was then raging in Europe — India deserved its own government.

This nationalist movement excited Nehru. To his father's astonishment, he joined the Allahabad branch of the Home Rule League. Now he was involved in an important political campaign working for Indian unity and freedom.

In February 1916, at the age of 26, Jawaharlal married Kamala Kaul, the wife his father had chosen for him. Kamala was the daughter of a prosperous Kashmiri businessman of the Brahman caste. Nehru's sister Krishna later described his bride as "16 years old and very lovely; slim and rather tall for an Indian girl, with typically fair skin of Brahmans of Kashmiri descent. Her hair was

This little man of poor physique had something of steel in him, something rock-like which did not yield to physical powers however great they might be.
—JAWAHARLAL NEHRU
on Mohandas K. Gandhi

dark brown and she had large brown eyes and a very gentle disposition."

Kamala was not as well educated as her husband. At first, Nehru felt they had very little in common. She had been raised in an Orthodox Hindu family and was not modern in her ways. But Nehru and Kamala overcame their differences, and in 1917 she gave birth to a child, a daughter whom the Nehrus called Indira.

In June 1917 Besant was imprisoned by the police to prevent her from making speeches and "stirring up trouble." People everywhere were outraged, including the Nehrus. How could the British authorities take such action against an elderly, white-haired lady? What crime had she committed?

Nehru found that he could not take his mind off Annie Besant's arrest. British attempts to silence her fueled his desire to become more involved in the independence movement. With his father's permission, Nehru gave up his law practice to devote his energies to the Home Rule League. He moved his family to Anand Bhawan to live with his parents. Motilal enjoyed having his children and grandchildren around him. He also agreed to support Nehru's family while the lawyer-turned-activist worked for the Indian nationalist cause.

All over India, people signed petitions demanding Annie Besant's release. Motilal Nehru was so angry about his friend's arrest that he joined the Home Rule League as a protest and would soon become the president of the division at Allahabad. Though not fully convinced that Gandhi's "noncooperation" with the British was the best way for Indians to gain their independence, Motilal, in his presidential address, declared satyagraha "a new force" with great power to change India's troubled situation. He admitted that Gandhi had won his countrymen's highest admiration. Yet Motilal stopped short of believing Congress could adopt Gandhi's strategy.

Conservative members of Congress were shocked, but his young activist son was immensely pleased. Nehru was also very proud that his father had cabled a letter of protest to British Prime Minister David Lloyd George in London. Motilal demanded to know

Gandhi as a young lawyer. After finishing his law studies in England, Gandhi practiced in South Africa during the 1890s. There he began leading protest movements to oppose the country's discrimination against the Indian community. In South Africa he first formulated his ideas of nonviolent resistance to oppression.

why England, which had such high regard for law and order at home, was using illegal methods of repression in India.

To ease the wave of tension that was surging through India, the British government released Annie Besant on September 17. The British hoped that by releasing Besant, the elderly revolutionary would fade out of politics. Instead, she quickly took advantage of her now widespread support and was elected president of the Indian National Congress.

Attempting to maintain some form of control over the situation, the British proposed several new policies that supposedly gave Indians greater freedom to govern themselves. The most important of these

Nehru with his wife, Kamala Kaul, and their daughter, Indira. At first Nehru resisted his arranged marriage to Kamala, believing that it conflicted with his modern ways. Fittingly, Indira grew up to be the embodiment of what many viewed as the new Indian woman.

policies promised self-government to the provinces after World War I ended. But in reality, no significant policy changes occurred. When World War I ended in 1918 the British viceroy, Frederic John Thesiger, Lord Chelmsford, retained governmental power in India.

Disappointed, and feeling cheated by the British, the Indian National Congress demanded a declaration of Indian independence. The British called the Congress's attitude "belligerent and arrogant" and tightened their legal restrictions on Indians.

In 1919 the British Parliament gave its officials in India the power to suppress all suspected political agitators. This piece of legislation was known as the Rowlatt Act. Many progressive Indians had expected the British to present a list of reforms. Instead, they were confronted with increased repression. In order to take the precautions the British believed necessary against possible terrorism, many legal procedures could be overlooked or skipped entirely under this act. The act took away the rights not only of India's few violent rebels but of every Indian. To lawyers, such as Nehru's father, this legislation was unconstitutional; Motilal called it "lawless." It made it legal for the British to arrest active supporters of the nationalist campaign, or anyone who spoke publicly about Indian independence.

To protest the unfair treatment by the British, Gandhi urged Indians everywhere to go on strike. The British viceroy, Lord Chelmsford, would not reverse the new repressive measures. In response to the Rowlatt Act, Gandhi created the organization known as *Satyagraha Sabha*. His answer to the Indian National Congress, which was searching for a solution to these laws, was peaceful resistance. Nehru was enthusiastic: he saw Gandhi's satyagraha as an effective way to fight back without taking up weapons against the British forces. Instead of going to work, Gandhi asked people to meet and pray for their enemies. He suggested that members of the Indian Congress not vote in elections sponsored by the British. He also advised his country's leaders to avoid British government schools and colleges. He asked all Indian lawyers, including Motilal Nehru, not to practice law in British-controlled courts.

Unlike previous Indian leaders, Gandhi's message appealed to many kinds of people — Indians from the Brahman caste (the highest class) to the lowest class of people, or *untouchables*, called that because no Hindu from another caste could touch them, or anything with which they came in contact, without polluting themselves. He spoke to rich and poor, peasants and princes, to Hindus, Muslims, and Sikhs (a religious community in northern India).

UPI/BETTMANN NEWSPHOTOS

Motilal Nehru, dressed in a homespun cotton robe. Outraged by Britain's repressive policies and pressured by Jawaharlal, Motilal became a follower of Gandhi. He gave up his law practice in 1920 to live the more simple, traditional life espoused by the Mahatma.

Gandhi was so respected that he was soon known as the *Mahatma*, or Great Soul.

At first, not everyone followed Gandhi. To many Congress members, Mahatma Gandhi was an eccentric — a strange man with peculiar ways. He wore very simple clothes, sometimes only a *dhoti*, or loincloth, wrapped around his waist and between his legs. In hot weather, the Mahatma was barechested. In cool weather, he wrapped himself in a plain white cloth. These clothes were made of cotton he had spun himself on a hand loom in order to protest the British-controlled textile industry. He ate only simple foods, mostly vegetables and milk, and frequently resorted to fasting as a means of protest. When his followers wondered whether they themselves should fast, Gandhi assured them that if their cause was ignored, then only he would suffer. Gandhi fasted to express purity in his love and devotion to humanity.

Indians in Bombay prepare to burn a British soldier in effigy. Among the tactics Gandhi advised for resisting the British were fasts, prayer, peaceful strikes, and boycotts of British goods and British-run law courts. He called his technique *satyagraha*, which means truth or "soul force."

UPI/BETTMANN NEWSPHOTOS

To Nehru, Gandhi's example was a heroic inspiration. The Mahatma almost magically led people to peacefully protest repression. Describing Gandhi in his autobiography, Nehru wrote, "We saw him functioning with success. It was so different from our method, which shouted a great deal and did little. Here was a man who didn't shout at all. He spoke gently and softly . . . there was . . . great strength about it." The Mahatma was a unifying force in a nation of diverse peoples who needed to work together for a free India.

In the past, the majority of Congress members had worked mainly for gradual government reform and a new constitution. But the Mahatma's gentle persuasiveness turned the tide. Now even "old guard" members of Congress recognized the value of Gandhi's methods. They decided to join his nonviolent protest campaign.

Next came the bloody massacre at Amritsar. The cruelty of General Dyer and his soldiers at Jallianwalla Bagh shocked the British Parliament, and

Followers of Gandhi behind bars in Lucknow prison, 1922. By this time, both the elder and younger Nehru were firmly committed to the Mahatma's leadership and ideals.

Impoverished Indian schoolchildren. Nehru's outlook was formed in part by the time he spent touring the country speaking to peasants. He came to believe that India needed a form of socialism to correct the widespread poverty and social inequities he witnessed.

General Dyer was dismissed from his command. But Britain's problem with colonial India was hardly at an end.

As the pace of the civil disobedience movement picked up and Nehru and his father got involved, 60-year-old Motilal changed his usual way of living. Like his son, he stopped wearing Western suits and clothes made of British cloth. He preferred homespun white cotton shirts and pants. Now he looked and felt more Indian. Sometimes Jawaharlal and Motilal slept on the floor as Gandhi did, to experience what it was like to live without common material comforts.

Dressed in loose pajamalike cotton pants, sandals, knee-length shirt, and a white cap, Nehru rallied volunteers to work for Gandhi's nonviolent resistance campaign. In doing so, he visited many rural villages and began to feel closer to poor farmers. Gently and sympathetically, Nehru encouraged rural peasants to peacefully disobey their landlords.

Sometimes Nehru stayed with the peasants for several days, sleeping in their mud huts and listening to them describe how they had been mistreated. He wept when he heard how many poor peasants had been beaten by their landlords and ruthlessly thrown off their land when they couldn't pay their taxes.

The squalor and misery of India's rural villages affected Nehru deeply. For the first time in his life he was embarrassed by wealth and luxury. He was angry that British-Indian politics had done so little for the multitudes of rural India. And he was filled with an overwhelming sense of responsibility. Nehru wanted to help the peasants. He wanted to work for Indian independence and end the poverty and suffering of India's poor.

Mohandas Gandhi, barechested and wearing his "dhoti," or loincloth (typical garb for hot weather). Though he came to win the hearts of Indians from all regions, castes, and faiths, he was regarded by some as an eccentric. Indeed, a popular refrain marveled: "What will Gandhi do next?"

3

Rising Young Leader

Throughout 1920 enthusiasm increased for Gandhi's campaign of civil disobedience. Wherever he went, thousands gathered to hear him preach his philosophy of peaceful resistance. Nehru, who had plunged heart and soul into Gandhi's campaign, continued to speak out for civil disobedience, encouraging others to join the movement. Motilal gave up his law practice this same year and devoted his energies to the independence movement. The slaughter at Amritsar, the jailing of Annie Besant, but mostly the dedication and enthusiasm of his son made Motilal support the radical nationalists, particularly Gandhi. Within a short time, he was targeted by the police as a troublemaker.

In May Nehru's sister Sarup was married to Ranjit Pandit, a young Allahabad lawyer. When peasants from nearby villages heard that Gandhi would attend the wedding ceremony at Anand Bhawan, thousands poured into Allahabad hoping to catch a glimpse of the Mahatma.

When local officials saw the huge crowds in Allahabad, and counted the number of Indian congressmen approaching Anand Bhawan, they expected

> *I became wholly absorbed in Gandhi's Non-Cooperation Movement. I gave up all my other associations and contacts, old friends, books, even newspapers, except articles concerned with the movement. I almost forgot my family, my wife, my daughter.*
> —JAWAHARLAL NEHRU

"India in chains" was the title of this political cartoon held aloft in a 1930 parade of Indian nationalists in Bombay. At the time, Nehru advocated swifter action to break the British shackles than either Gandhi or his own father thought the Indian people were ready for.

trouble. They suspected that the wedding celebration was merely an excuse for conspirators from all over India to meet and plan a revolt.

As a precaution, police and secret service men surrounded the Nehru mansion on Sarup's wedding day. But the celebration proceeded without incident, and Nehru's sister became Vijaya Laksmi Pandit.

Gandhi's popularity worried the British, as did the fact that so many Indian congressmen joined his civil disobedience campaign. The British feared losing control of India. Now the viceroy decided that something had to be done to weaken Gandhi's position.

To upstage the Mahatma and minimize the importance of Congress's campaign activities, the viceroy planned a spectacular royal celebration in India. Prince Edward, heir to the British throne, made a goodwill tour of India. To honor the prince, the British organized splendid processions and royal parades in every major city. Indians everywhere would be impressed with the power and majesty of the British Empire.

But Gandhi, Congress, and the Nehrus planned a less spectacular kind of welcome for the prince. On November 17, 1921, the day Prince Edward arrived in Bombay, he was surrounded by groups of angry demonstrators chanting anti-British slogans. Gandhi had proclaimed a nationwide strike, and thousands had responded to his call. There were no cheering crowds for Prince Edward.

The massive demonstrations against the prince embarrassed and humiliated British officials. They struck back hard. Following the demonstrations, they arrested almost 30,000 nationalists. They also jailed many prominent Indian congressmen. In December both Jawaharlal and Motilal Nehru were arrested and sentenced to six months at the Lucknow District Jail.

This was the first of many such arrests for Nehru. During his lifetime he spent a total of nine years in jail. Nehru believed, as Gandhi did, that going to jail was the most effective way he could fight British oppression. Speaking on his own behalf at his trial,

Nehru echoed Gandhi's manner, style, and ideas.

The people of India soon recognized in young Nehru the qualities of a great national leader. He was a man willing to sacrifice his personal freedom and material comforts on his countrymen's behalf. His courage and determination were an inspiration to others, and he never wavered in his dedication to the cause of Indian independence.

Life in prison was not easy for Nehru or his father. Their cells were tiny, damp, and full of insects. Motilal, who was old and sick, had difficulty breathing in his small, stuffy cell. The food was all but inedible.

During the years he spent in prison, Nehru tried to use his time well. He kept his mind active by reading and writing. He became the author of several books. These include *Glimpses of World History* (1934); *Jawaharlal Nehru — An Autobiography* (1936); *Toward Freedom* (1941); and *The Discovery of India* (1946).

Gandhi as he appeared in 1931. Gandhi was so fanatically worshiped that his legs were often covered with scratches from people trying to touch him.

In his writing, Nehru described his philosophy, political ideas, and his hopes for India's future. He envisioned his homeland as a free nation, able to produce enough food to feed its impoverished masses. He looked forward to a time when India's various religious groups could live together in harmony. Nehru believed none of this could happen under British rule. He knew the struggle for independence had to continue.

After his release from Lucknow prison, Nehru was arrested again and jailed in Nabha prison. Describing his experience in Nabha, Nehru wrote, "It [the cell] was small and damp, with a low ceiling which we could almost touch. At night we slept on the floor and I would wake up with a start, full of horror, to find that a rat or mouse had just passed over my face." There he contracted typhoid fever, and the authorities suspended his sentence. He returned to Allahabad, where he recovered from his illness.

After his imprisonment at Lucknow, Nehru realized that Congress had been divided. The radical supporters of Gandhi and civil disobedience made up one faction. The other faction, of which Nehru's father was an important leader, believed in fighting the British by legal, constitutional means — working for change within the system. Those still dedicated to Gandhi's methods were led by three men who

British policemen disperse Indian nationalist demonstrators. When the noncooperation movement broke out in violence in the early 1920s, Gandhi suspended it. Subsequently, he was arrested by the British and sentenced to six years in jail for sedition — attempting to overthrow British rule.

would remain significant throughout the independence struggle. They were Rajaji, Rajendra Prasad, and Sardar Vallabhbhai Patel. Nehru did not want to join either group. Although being in prison did not convince Motilal to abandon Gandhi's principles completely, he felt certain compromises were needed. In 1922 he helped organize the Swaraj party. Three years later, this party fell apart under attack from other parties.

In 1926 Nehru's wife, Kamala, contracted tuberculosis. Doctors recommended a trip to Switzerland for treatment by better physicians. In March the Nehrus sailed to Europe with eight-year-old Indira. Nehru's sister Krishna accompanied them to help care for Kamala.

They settled in Geneva, where Indira was enrolled in a Swiss school and Kamala could receive medical treatment. At that time, Geneva served as headquarters for the League of Nations. The league was established in 1920, in the aftermath of World War I, to promote cooperation and peace among the world's nations.

In Geneva, Nehru attended several lectures at the Geneva School for International Studies. He met and talked with many world statesmen and diplomats who taught at the school. They discussed dif-

Followers of Gandhi's satyagraha movement are released from jail in 1922. Activists set free by the British were greeted by their fellow nationalists and each was given a huge handkerchief made of homespun "Gandhi cloth" as a reward for their great heroism.

I see no way of ending the poverty, the vast unemployment, the degradation and the subjection of the Indian people except through socialism.
—JAWAHARLAL NEHRU

41

ferent political points of view and forms of government, including socialism and communism. Nehru was particularly interested in socialism, a system whereby everyone in the community, or the country, works and then distributes equally what is produced. Such a system also requires that major industries be the property of the state. He thought a socialist economy in India might solve the problem of wealthy landowners who mistreated their peasant farm workers.

Nehru's experiences in Geneva broadened his thinking. He developed an international view. He saw India not only as a nation to be freed from British rule but also as a country that belonged to the world community of nations. Nehru wanted an independent India to participate in world affairs. The principles of national independence, noninterference in the affairs of other nations, and peaceful coexistence were ones that Nehru would support throughout his political career. He also advocated "nonalignment," or avoiding taking sides in conflicts between major world powers.

When Kamala was well enough, Nehru left her under Krishna's care and traveled throughout Europe. He visited several countries, including France, Italy, Germany, the Soviet Union, and Belgium. In Brussels, he was invited to give a speech at an anti-imperialist conference. His speech impressed everyone. He talked about how destructive British imperialism was to India. This was the first time Nehru had addressed an audience of world statesmen and dignitaries. Their response gave him new confidence in his ability to give his political ideals expression before an international group. Now Nehru felt better prepared to fight for Indian independence.

The Nehrus returned to India in 1927. The boat docked in Madras, where the Indian National Congress was in session. Nehru, a member of the Congress Working Committee, went directly to the meeting. He was full of energy and enthusiasm for a free India and immediately introduced a resolution to Congress. Nehru asked the members to approve a resolution for complete independence from Britain. This resolution was more extreme than the

Home Rule resolution Congress had previously passed. Home Rule meant India would gradually develop its own self-government under British control. But Nehru's resolution called for breaking all ties with Britain and giving total freedom to India. To Nehru's amazement, the majority in Congress approved his resolution.

But Motilal and Gandhi, both powerful leaders in Congress, disagreed with Jawaharlal's resolution. They recommended moving more slowly and cautiously against the British. Motilal favored a new constitution for India, one that would ensure self-rule, but he did not want to cut all ties with Britain. He preferred keeping India's status as a dominion, meaning that the nation would remain linked to the

Gandhi (with towel on head) participates in a peaceful demonstration. After serving two years of the prison sentence for sedition he received in 1922, Gandhi was released to discover India's nationalist movement in shambles. Announcing a 21-day program of fasting and spinning, Gandhi hoped to stop the organization's infighting. Nehru emerged as the Mahatma's most prominent disciple.

Stamp used by India's nationalists to commemorate the Gandhi-inspired "boycott week" of July 1930. The stamp at lower left bears a portrait of the British monarch, King George V.

rest of the British Empire. Gandhi now wanted to avoid angry confrontations with the British and thought that demanding immediate independence would result in violence. The Mahatma also thought it would take time for India's peasants to understand radical changes.

As the 1929 election year approached, significant differences in the political thinking among Congress's leading candidates began to emerge. The members of Congress had to decide whom to elect as their next president. They were forced to choose among Gandhi, Nehru, or the elder Nehru, Motilal. All three were respected leaders. Almost all the younger members supported the young Nehru; the older members, his father. But the majority of Congress seemed to prefer India's popular spiritual leader, Mahatma Gandhi.

When Gandhi heard that Congress might elect him president, he declined the nomination and asked his supporters to vote for Nehru instead. Gandhi, now 60, realized he was getting old, and he knew that India's future depended on the will and energy of its youth. He also knew that the educated young people of India saw Jawaharlal Nehru as their leader. Therefore, Gandhi wanted Nehru to become India's next leader. Despite their political differences, the Mahatma respected many of Nehru's ideas and knew that he had the ability to lead the nation. Above all, he trusted Nehru's intelligence and his devotion to the people of India.

Just before the election, Gandhi made a speech to Congress praising Nehru: "In bravery, he is not to be surpassed. Who can excel him in the love of the country. . . . And if he has the . . . rashness of a warrior, he has also the prudence of a statesman. . . . He is as pure as crystal, he is truthful beyond suspicion. . . . The nation is safe in his hands."

On Christmas Day in 1929 the Indian National Congress elected Jawaharlal Nehru as its president. His inaugural address sounded very much like a declaration of independence. "Violence," he said, "is bad, but slavery is worse." He reminded the people of India that it takes great courage to act and that timid people who are afraid to stand up for their principles are rarely successful.

As he ended his speech, thunderous applause filled the room. The members of Congress stood and cheered for Nehru, their new president. A few days later, the Indian National Congress unanimously voted to fight for complete independence from the British Empire. Nehru's triumph in the Congress was his first major breakthrough in national politics. Years later, recalling the 1929 Congress, he wrote, "If we did not actually gain independence in that year, at least our hearts became free."

UPI/BETTMANN NEWSPHOTOS

May God spare you for many a long year to come and make you his chosen instrument in freeing India from the yoke.
—MOHANDAS K. GANDHI giving his blessing in 1929 to Nehru's aspirations toward the presidency of the Indian Congress

Nationalists parade in Bombay in 1930. In December 1929 Nehru was elected president of the Indian National Congress. It was his first major triumph in national politics and marked the beginning of a new era in India's fight for independence.

4

The Struggle for Independence

The Indian National Congress declared January 26, 1930, as Independence Day, although independence had not actually been won. Imbued with new confidence, Congress, headed by Nehru, pledged to free India from British rule. All over the country Indians gathered solemnly to recite the Indian declaration of independence, which began with the following words, echoing the American Declaration of Independence:

"We believe that it is the inalienable right of the Indian people . . . to have freedom and to enjoy the fruits of their life . . . and that if any government deprives a people of these rights and oppresses them, the people have a further right to alter it or abolish it."

Nehru and Gandhi were pleased that so many people had participated in the Independence Day celebration.

To gain support for the national independence campaign, Gandhi organized another mass disobedience movement. He had to find a universal issue

Jawaharlal Nehru realized better than most leaders of India's nationalist movement that without struggle there could be no independence.
—TARIQ ALI
Indian historian

Nehru in the 1930s. Even after ascending to the Congress's leadership, and despite some differences with Gandhi, Nehru continued to take his cues from the Mahatma. As he once wrote to Gandhi, "Who am I to argue with a magician?"

to protest, something simple that everyone understood. He knew that salt was commonly used throughout the country. It was consumed by almost every Indian, from the wealthiest Brahman to the poorest untouchable. So the Mahatma decided to protest the Salt Act, which guaranteed British profits from the sale of salt manufactured in India. Salt was in great demand and very marketable. Now Gandhi announced that no Indian should buy salt or pay the salt tax. Instead, he told the Indian people to make salt themselves by evaporating seawater, which produced salt as a residue. Gandhi knew such an action was unlawful: the production of salt was a British monopoly.

Gandhi planned a long march through India covering 241 miles, traveling from village to village. He would walk from Ahmadabad, in northwest India, to the village of Dandi, on the shore of the Arabian

Women activists taking part in protests against British rule in 1930.

Sea in the southwest, where there were crude salt deposits.

Before he began the Salt March, Gandhi contacted Edward F. L. Wood, Lord Irwin, the British viceroy since 1925, and promised to cancel the march if the viceroy changed certain unfair government practices. The changes he asked for included reducing land taxes, abolishing the salt tax, and releasing political prisoners from jail. But the viceroy paid no attention.

Thus, the 60-year-old Mahatma began his walking crusade early in March. Frail and thin, the bare-legged old man plodded along in the blazing sun. His silver-rimmed eyeglasses sparkled in the sunlight as he moved along the dusty roads, passing thousands of people who lined the route. Now and then he stopped to rest or recite a prayer with his followers. As the Mahatma passed, people reached out to touch his hand or offer him a cup of water.

Gandhi walked for several weeks. Hundreds joined him along the way. Wherever he went, thousands cheered him from the sidelines. Newspapers all over the world carried stories about Mahatma Gandhi's dramatic Salt March. His courage and determination inspired millions of Indians and caught the attention of the world.

His walking crusade attracted thousands of followers. Along the route, Gandhi preached his message of nonviolence. And while Gandhi walked, Nehru directed and organized the civil disobedience campaign from Congress's headquarters.

On April 5, 1930, the Mahatma and his loyal disciples arrived at Dandi on the sea. There Gandhi picked up a tiny amount of the crude salt lying on the beach and held it in his hand. This was a signal to the masses — a symbolic act of defiance against the British. Gandhi was telling the Indian people to boycott salt produced by the British, thus avoiding British taxation while protesting against unfair British policies.

The Salt March succeeded overwhelmingly, and the protest movement gained momentum. Now there was no turning back. Nehru organized what ultimately became an economic boycott of all un-

The law of life should not be acquisitiveness, but cooperation, the good of each contributing to the good of all.
—JAWAHARLAL NEHRU

Satyagraha demonstrators (including Gandhi's wife, at extreme left) participate in the famed Salt March, held from March to April 1930. Seeking a new target for resistance, the 61-year-old Gandhi led a 24-day, 241-mile trek to the sea, where he picked up a few grains of salt in defiance of the British monopoly on salt production.

fairly taxed Indian products and British goods sold in India.

Throughout the summer, Indians picketed textile and crafts shops selling goods taxed by the British government. In another form of protest, some people deliberately lay down in city streets, obstructing traffic and refusing to move even on the command of the police.

Early in April, Nehru addressed more than a million people at public gatherings. He urged them to join the campaign. For the first time, many women participated, including Kamala Nehru. Her husband was proud when she helped organize groups to picket cloth shops.

Massive strikes occurred in major cities, including Bombay and Calcutta. And wherever the demonstrations took place, the police arrested the

"agitators." Nehru was among them. The British thought that by jailing Indian Congress leaders, including Nehru, the Congress's president, they could bring the protest movement to a halt. This time Nehru was jailed for several months and kept in solitary confinement. By June both Gandhi and Motilal Nehru had also been arrested.

The people of India were angry that their national leaders had been jailed. The British colonial viceroy, Lord Irwin, feared that continued Indian resentment might cause a revolution. He sent a representative to the prison to see what could be done to relieve the tension.

Indian women boil seawater to obtain salt rather than purchase British-produced salt. At a subsequent salt march held while Gandhi was in prison for breaking the salt laws, some 2,500 satyagrahi marching on the Dharsana Salt Works were struck down by British policemen wielding weighted clubs. None of the marchers raised so much as an arm to fend off the blows.

> *The French Revolution of 150 years ago gradually ushered in an age of political equality, but the times have changed and that by itself is not enough today. The boundaries of democracy have to be widened now so as to include economic equality also. This is the great revolution through which we are all passing.*
>
> —JAWAHARLAL NEHRU

Nehru agreed to talk to Lord Irwin. Nehru promised to suspend the civil disobedience activities if all political prisoners were released. He also demanded that Britain acknowledge India's right to secede, or separate, from Britain. A temporary agreement was reached. Within a short time, Nehru, his father, and Gandhi were released from jail.

But before the first anniversary of Indian Independence Day arrived, Nehru was jailed again. He had defied a court order prohibiting him from speaking in public. While he was in jail, his ailing father took over for him in Congress. To call attention to the freedom campaign, Motilal arranged a nationwide celebration of Nehru's birthday on November 14. Huge crowds gathered at the Congress assembly to hear a congressman read Nehru's speeches. In Allahabad, Kamala celebrated her husband's birthday by reading the speech Nehru gave on the day he was arrested. She, too, was briefly jailed. Still in prison, Nehru learned of Kamala's bravery, but he also received word that his father was gravely ill.

On January 26, 1931, the first anniversary of Indian Independence Day, Nehru was released early from prison. He rushed to Allahabad to be with his sick father. Motilal was very weak, barely able to speak. Nehru sat by his father's bedside and talked to him quietly about all the experiences they had shared in the struggle for freedom. Motilal was proud of the work they had done together. Motilal died on February 6, 1931. Describing his father on his deathbed, Nehru later wrote, "There he sat, like an old lion mortally wounded and with his physical strength almost gone, but still very . . . kingly."

After Motilal's death, Nehru went to the island of Ceylon (now called Sri Lanka) with Kamala and Indira for a brief rest. When he returned to India, British authorities ordered him not to leave Allahabad and again ordered him not to make public speeches.

While in Allahabad, Nehru learned that a wave of terrorism had erupted in the province of Bengal, in the northeast. Peasants who couldn't pay their rent were rebelling over harsh treatment by the author-

UPI/BETTMANN NEWSPHOTOS

ities. Nehru's help was needed. Congress called an emergency meeting in Bombay, and Nehru decided to attend. But the police were waiting for him as he stepped off the train in Bombay. He was arrested, tried, and sentenced to two years in Dehra Dun prison on the charge of violating a court order forbidding him to leave Allahabad. Unbowed by this misfortune, Nehru wrote, "Perhaps the happiest place for me is the gaol [jail]! I have another three months here before I go out, and one can always return."

Demonstrators in 1930 rally to protest Gandhi's arrest. Rather than quell the uprisings and nationalist sentiments, the British incarceration of Gandhi, Nehru, and other Congress leaders only intensified demands for Britain to vacate the country.

Nehru and his father in Allahabad prison in 1930. When not fending off the insects and rodents, Nehru tried to use his time in prison to consolidate his thoughts regarding India's future. Meanwhile, his father's health was ruined by his term in jail, and Motilal died, shortly after his release, on February 6, 1931.

During 1932–33, while Nehru was incarcerated, the struggle for independence took another turn. In May 1933 Gandhi began a 21-day "fast unto death" to protest a proposal made by the British that the Mahatma believed was harmful to the untouchables of India.

The British prime minister, Ramsay MacDonald, had proposed that a new Indian constitution include a provision, called the Communal Award, for minority groups. This meant that the various religious elements or communities within India, including the untouchables, would be treated as separate voting groups. Gandhi opposed the idea. He believed that treating the untouchables separately was immoral and discriminatory. He wanted the untouchables to have equal voting rights, with each vote having equal weight, in deciding whether to accept the proposed constitution.

Gandhi had worked hard to improve the status of untouchables. They were required to do all the low-level labor in India, including cleaning the streets and picking up dead animals. Shunned by all other Hindus, the untouchables were not allowed to eat, bathe, or walk with them. There were separate wells for the untouchables, who were forced to live outside the villages. Gandhi wanted to give the untouchables equal status and dignity in India. To honor the untouchables and show them respect, the Mahatma renamed them *harijans*, or "children of God."

British troops, with the help of Indian native police, disperse nationalist protesters in Peshawar in July 1930. Some of the Indian troops were arrested after refusing to charge a procession of Gandhi's supporters, sparking huge protests elsewhere in the country.

Gandhi again emerges from incarceration. The British viceroy, Lord Irwin, released Gandhi from prison in early 1931 because he feared that the Indian leader's continued imprisonment would only further inflame the public and possibly lead to an outright revolution.

When Nehru heard about Gandhi's fast, he was upset and confused. He wondered why Gandhi had strayed from the issue of Indian unity and independence. Was the problem of the untouchables essential to the freedom struggle? Moreover, Nehru worried about Gandhi's fast. He was afraid the Mahatma might die. From jail, he wrote to his daughter Indira, "Shall I not see him again? Whom shall I go to when I am in doubt and require wise counsel?"

Gandhi continued his fast, almost to the point of death. His friends and followers begged him to stop. A group of Hindu Congress leaders met at his bedside to discuss a possible solution. But Gandhi would not listen. Five more days passed, and the Mahatma refused to eat.

Finally, the British government agreed to a compromise. They were afraid that if Gandhi died, India would revolt. Under the proposed new constitution, the British agreed to exclude the separate division for untouchable voters. Gandhi called off his fast, and Indians everywhere breathed a sigh of relief. But the struggle with the British for independence had only just begun.

Nehru delivering a speech before an Indian nationalist crowd. He and Gandhi spent much of the early 1930s in jail, during which time Gandhi staged hunger strikes to gain more legal rights for India's lowest social class, the "untouchables." Meanwhile, Nehru was furthering the cause of India's independence by negotiating concessions from the British.

5

Unity and Separatism

Toward the end of 1933, Nehru was released from prison, but he faced difficult months ahead. His mother was critically ill, and Kamala's health was deteriorating. And Gandhi, who was like a second father to him, seemed to be moving in a different political direction from Indian Home Rule. Nehru was becoming impatient with Gandhi's spiritualist approach to political issues. At that time, the Mahatma's advice seemed impractical. Now the two leaders often disagreed about campaign strategies and tactics.

Gandhi was convinced that the method used to achieve freedom was as important as freedom itself. To the Mahatma, freedom was not worth violence and bloodshed. Nehru disagreed, although he preferred nonviolence. "If methods of violence will rid us of slavery, then I . . . will adopt them," he said.

Nehru's days in prison coincided with his search for a solid political program for India. He not only wanted to see India freed from British domination, but believed that India needed a specific political and economic system once independence was achieved. He soon found that he could not agree

Whither India? Surely to the great human goal of social and economic equality, to the ending of exploitation of nation by nation and class by class, to national freedom within the framework of an international cooperative socialist world federation.
—JAWAHARLAL NEHRU
in his 1933 pamphlet,
Whither India

Nehru speaks in London in the late 1930s. Increasingly confident after being reelected as president of the Indian National Congress in 1937, Nehru disagreed more frequently with the Mahatma's tactics, at one point saying that "violence is bad, but slavery is far worse."

with Gandhi on many issues. One of these was socialism, an idea that Nehru had discovered earlier while reading and studying in prison. He studied the writings of the 19th-century social philosopher Karl Marx. According to Marx, socialism would replace the capitalist system, which would be overthrown by the working class, or "proletariat." In theory, society's wealth would then be distributed equally, rather than unequally among the richer and poorer classes. To Nehru, Marx "surveyed past history as a scientist and drew certain conclusions from it."

Nehru was bitterly opposed to fascism — the brutal, dictatorial governments of Adolf Hitler in Germany and Benito Mussolini in Italy. But the Soviet Union's rigid communist system (founded by the Russian Marxist revolutionary Vladimir Lenin) also

In a rickety bamboo chariot drawn by six festively adorned bulls, Nehru makes his way through the streets for the ceremonies marking his reinstallation as president of the Indian National Congress in 1937.

did not appeal to Nehru. He did not want India to imitate any other country's government. In addition, Nehru understood that unity among all Indians, whether rich or poor, was vital to gaining independence. A struggle between India's classes could easily destroy the nation's chances for freedom. As his thinking became more radical, however, he found he could no longer accept Gandhi's more religious viewpoint and stated, "Our objectives are different, our ideas different, our spiritual outlook is different. . . ."

In 1935 Britain introduced the new constitution to India. The country would now be ruled by an equal representative state council and a proportionally representative assembly. Political parties could now coalesce into real electoral powers. The Indian National Congress continued to function but also forged a new "Congress party" in order to participate in the government. Despite his sympathy for the socialists' ideas, such as organizing peasants and workers against the British, Nehru could not support the goal of the All-India Congress Socialist party. Making the Congress accept socialist principles could damage its popularity with the Indian people. Nevertheless, Nehru continued to receive the socialists' overwhelming support. Gandhi, seeing Nehru's importance to the campaign for independence, would endorse him later, in 1936, to lead the Congress as its president. Nehru worked with dedication to promote unity and refused to give in to any one side's demands.

Imprisoned again in 1935, Nehru learned that Kamala's doctors advised her to return to Europe for treatment, and he sent a telegram to his 17-year-old daughter, Indira, asking her to take Kamala to a special hospital in Germany.

By August Kamala's condition was critical. British authorities felt sorry for Nehru and released him from prison so he could join his wife and daughter in Europe. When Nehru saw Kamala, he was heartbroken. He knew his wife was dying.

Kamala, realizing she did not have long to live, made her last requests to her husband. She asked Jawaharlal to enroll Indira in an English school. She

> *[Soviet] Communism became too closely associated with the necessity for violence and thus the idea which it placed before the world became a tainted one. Means distorted ends.*
> —JAWAHARLAL NEHRU

also asked him to go to London to arrange to publish his autobiography, which he had recently finished. They had spent many hours together discussing the book, and Nehru had read many pages of it aloud to his wife. Kamala was proud of her husband and knew his book was important. It was about India and its struggle for freedom. Nehru promised to honor Kamala's requests. She died peacefully on February 28, 1936.

In 1937 the Indian National Congress reelected Nehru as its president. On receiving this news, Nehru felt no joy. Now that Kamala was gone, he was nearly overcome by grief and sorrow. As a memorial to his wife, the autobiography he wrote is dedicated to her. The inscription reads: "To Kamala, who is no more."

To many people in India, Nehru began to appear much older after Kamala's death. His sister Krishna wrote, "His face which had . . . looked so youthful, was aged and lined with sorrow." Despite his grief, Nehru returned to his responsibilities and the duties of his office. A friend from his days in England cheered Nehru on, telling him, "Don't undervalue yourself in this hour of misery. India has great need of you — especially, personally, of you. . . . Try to draw strength from the belief that history has named you to lead." As before, in moments of despair, he found consolation in his work — the struggle for Indian freedom. Pressured by conservatives, progressives, and socialists, Nehru managed to remain independent in his thinking. Events that began in 1937, the year he was reelected president of the Congress, required all his energy.

A popular Congress president, Nehru toured the country urging his countrymen to join the Congress party. The larger the party, the better able it would be to fight for India's freedom. Nehru traveled by plane, train, and automobile. To reach peasants in remote villages, he sometimes traveled on foot, by bicycle, or on the back of an elephant. His campaign focused on land reforms and lowering rents and taxes for poor farmers.

Winning the election gave Nehru renewed confidence, and his efforts began to show results. Soon

Nehru meets with Chinese Nationalist leader Chiang Kai-shek and his wife, Madame Chiang, during a tour of China in 1939. Nehru's trips abroad contributed to his political outlook, which emphasized international tolerance and cooperation.

the Congress party became the most powerful political party in India. In the 1937 election, even many Muslims voted for the Congress party, and not for its major opponent — Mohammed Ali Jinnah's Muslim League.

"There are only two forces in India today," said Nehru in a victory speech to Congress, "British imperialism, and Indian nationalism as represented by Congress!" Nehru's remark offended Jinnah. He resented Nehru's overconfident attitude. It seemed to Jinnah that Nehru was ignoring India's Muslims. "No," declared Jinnah, "there is a third party . . . the Muslims!"

Although discord and suspicion between Hindus and Muslims had existed in India for many years, Nehru's popularity and the growing strength of the

Nehru (upper left) greets a crowd from the doorway of his second-class railway compartment. As the Congress's president, Nehru made extensive forays into the countryside to enlist new Congress party supporters. Like most independence leaders, Nehru and Gandhi chose to ride in second- and third-class cars with their peasant following.

predominantly Hindu Congress party disturbed Jinnah. Muslims comprised 30 percent of India's population but had few representatives in the British-Indian assembly. Jinnah did not trust Nehru and the Congress party. He feared that if India won its independence under Nehru's leadership, Muslims would be denied government jobs. Jinnah was convinced that under the Congress party, Muslims would be controlled by Hindus instead of by the British.

Jinnah decided to oppose Indian nationalism, Nehru, and the Congress party. He decided to campaign for Muslim unity and make the Muslim League a more powerful political group. He wanted Muslim voices heard and their interests protected. To arouse his people, Jinnah toured the country shouting a warning slogan to Muslim peasants: "Islam is in danger! . . . Islam is in danger!" Jinnah's

chant had the sound of a war cry. From then on, antagonism between Hindus and Muslims increased steadily. Jinnah's campaign was successful. He eventually became the spokesman for more than 90 million Indian Muslims.

While violent confrontations were taking place between Muslim and Hindu mobs, World War II erupted in Europe in 1939. In September Hitler, Germany's Nazi dictator, invaded Poland and threatened to take over all of Europe. Great Britain declared war on Germany, and without discussing it with Indian leaders, the British viceroy announced that India was also at war with Germany.

This announcement enraged the members of Congress. Nehru, who had been away touring China, immediately returned to India to meet with the Congress Working Committee. They had to consider India's role in the war. Was India prepared to fight for Britain as it had during World War I?

Nehru hated the fascists and wanted to see Hitler defeated, but he was determined to continue the struggle for Indian independence. He argued to Congress that Indians had the right to make their own choice about fighting with the British. Nehru realized that Britain needed India's help in the war. Japan, which had come under the control of a military dictatorship during the 1930s, had set out to create its own vast empire in Asia. Japan's armies had seized parts of China; their long-range objectives were to capture British Malaya, Burma, the Dutch East Indies, and the Philippines. By 1937 the Japanese militarists posed a gigantic threat to Southeast Asia. In five years, Japan would capture Singapore (the capital of British Malaya) and the city of Rangoon in Burma. These victories would bring Japanese forces dangerously close to India.

Now India was in a powerful position to negotiate with Britain for Indian freedom. Congress debated the issue. Gandhi, still the dedicated pacifist, argued against India and Britain taking violent action. He thought Hitler could be defeated through "spiritual force" and a campaign of nonviolent resistance. Nehru disagreed and won the debate. On September 14, 1939, Congress passed a resolution

Mohammed Ali Jinnah, the leader of the Muslim League and of India's 90 million Muslims, in 1942. Once India achieved independence, Jinnah wanted the nation divided into separate Muslim and Hindu states, directly in conflict with Nehru's dream of a united and free India.

A trained elephant hoists a 55-gallon fuel drum onto a transport plane in India during World War II. Without discussing the matter with Indian authorities, in 1939 Britain declared that India was also at war with Hitler's Germany. Resentful of yet another colonial decree, the Congress said it would support Britain if granted independence after World War II.

to support Britain in the war, with the condition that Britain would immediately prepare to transfer governmental power to India. A week after the resolution was passed, the British viceroy invited India's leaders to come to London to discuss a transfer of power.

The Muslim League sent Jinnah to represent India's Muslims at the meeting. Britain now recognized Jinnah as the powerful head of the Muslim League. Jinnah's campaign for Muslim unity had worked. With a strong voice, Jinnah now spoke for India's Muslims. Jinnah wanted Muslims to leave India and form their own separate country under his leadership.

The Indian National Congress sent Nehru to negotiate for them at the London meetings. Nehru was hopeful. Was it possible that his dream of freedom for India might become a reality?

When Nehru began to explain Congress's point of view at the London meeting, the British viceroy rudely interrupted him, saying, "A little more slowly, Mr. Nehru, my slow Anglo-Saxon mind cannot keep

pace with your quick intellect." Then, referring to Jinnah and the Muslim League, the viceroy suggested that a governmental transfer could not take place until the Muslims were completely satisfied with all conditions.

Nehru, insulted by the viceroy's remark and furious with Jinnah's lack of cooperation, appealed directly to Jinnah: "I do not know what you and your colleagues in the Muslim League will decide . . . but I trust you will express your strong disapproval of the viceroy's statement and refuse to cooperate with him. . . . I feel strongly that our dignity and self-respect as Indians have been insulted by the British Government."

Jinnah glared at Nehru and said nothing. Indian nationalism was not his concern, and the viceroy had not insulted him. On the contrary, Jinnah was happy that the viceroy appeared to recognize that there were now two nations in India, one Hindu and one Muslim. At the London meeting, Jawaharlal Nehru's dream of Indian unity and freedom suddenly became a nightmare.

An army mule is forced onto a transport plane, carrying supplies for air commandoes near the India-Burma border in 1944. The Japanese, whose troops captured much of China and occupied parts of Southeast Asia, were defeated before they could invade India.

6

Turning Points

The British Parliament had discussed the issue of Indian independence almost continually during the two decades between the world wars. India, once Britain's most important colonial possession, was becoming too difficult to control and maintain. Britain could no longer afford to help sustain India's growing population of about 350 million people, many of them poor, uneducated peasants.

In time, the British would favor more Indian independence. But by 1939 Britain had still not made a final decision about when or how to transfer complete governmental power to its colony. Several problems stood in the way. After occupying India for almost 200 years, could the empire find a dignified way to let go of this valuable colony?

The British government worried that giving up the largest, most populated colony in its empire would reduce its prestige and power in the world. Britain's pride was at stake. Although Stanley Baldwin, the influential Conservative party leader in Parliament, had accepted the eventual need for India's independence in 1931, many British statesmen flatly rejected this idea. One of them was Winston

If I were given the chance to go through my life again, with my present knowledge and experiences, my major decisions on public affairs would remain untouched.
—JAWAHARLAL NEHRU
writing from Dehra Dun
prison, 1940

Nehru on February 21, 1947, the morning after the British government announced that it would withdraw from India in June 1948. At the time, India was torn by a near civil war between Hindus and Muslims, the nation's two chief religious groups.

> *Prison is the best of universities if only one knows how to take its courses. Physically of course one has the chance of regular and simple living. Mentally, its effect is still more noteworthy. Our age is the Age of Indifference. People have no real beliefs left — nothing sacred — nothing worthwhile almost. And so we suffer from ennui and life itself becomes a burden. We have lost entirely our sense of perspective — well, jail gives it back to us to some extent and we begin to appreciate the little things, which we hardly noticed before.*
> —JAWAHARLAL NEHRU

Churchill, who became British prime minister in 1940. Churchill became notorious for his stubborn opposition to the Indian independence movement. He considered it a disgrace to the empire to lose India. He and his supporters described India as the "jewel in the Crown" of the British Empire. It also was unclear who would govern India after the British *raj* (rule) withdrew from the great subcontinent. There appeared to be only three possibilities. The new independent regime could be formed either by Nehru's Congress party or Jinnah's Muslim League, while the third possibility was that the rulers of the princely states would regain control.

Although Nehru was not aware of it, when the viceroy invited him to London for "frank and free" discussions about a transfer of power, Britain had no intention of immediately granting India independence. He soon discovered that the meetings were used merely as another delaying tactic to calm things down and put off the final decision.

Embittered and discouraged, Nehru returned to India and decided to do things Gandhi's way. He agreed to help the Mahatma lead another mass civil disobedience campaign. But within a short time, Nehru was arrested and charged with "antigovernment propaganda." It was difficult for Nehru to face imprisonment for the eighth time without being depressed. From his jail cell in Dehra Dun, the dejected Nehru wrote, "The years I have spent in prison! Sitting alone, wrapped up in my thoughts, how many seasons I have seen go by, following one another into oblivion . . . sometimes I see the ghosts of dead yesterdays rise up . . . and whispering to me . . . they say, 'Was it worthwhile?' " He thought, too, of his mother, Swaruprani, who had died not long before. Now his wife and both his parents were dead. In prison, his loneliness became almost unbearable.

On December 7, 1941, three days after Nehru was released from prison, the Japanese attacked Pearl Harbor, Hawaii. It was here that the United States had stationed its fleet in the Pacific Ocean. As part of a major offensive in the Pacific, the Japanese naval aircraft sank 19 U.S. ships. The Japanese also struck simultaneously at Thailand, Malaya, and Lu-

Gandhi as he appeared in the late 1940s. During World War II Gandhi launched his "Quit India" campaign to speed the departure of the British from India. This strategy failed, resulting only in his own arrest, and increased tensions among the country's various ethnic and religious groups.

Crowds jam the streets of Bombay to welcome Nehru upon his release from his longest term in prison: August 1942 to August 1945. With Gandhi imprisoned for two years at the same time, Congress and the independence movement were virtually without leadership, and the country descended into chaos.

zon (the main island of the Philippines). Following this attack, the United States declared war on Japan on December 8. Three days later, Japan's allies, Germany and Italy, declared war on the United States. World War II had suddenly escalated. The Japanese army moved through Southeast Asia and threatened to invade India. The British army fighting in Burma was forced to retreat. With the Japanese almost at India's border, the British army needed help. In London, the government decided to renew negotiations with India. This time, in March 1942, they sent Sir Stafford Cripps to meet with Indian leaders to discuss independence. The leader of the British House of Commons (one of the two houses that make up the British Parliament), Cripps had visited India three years earlier to explore possibilities for a journey to India by members of Parliament. Cripps was respected by the Muslim League and by Congress's leaders, including Nehru. Nehru was also favorably impressed by the fact that Cripps was a socialist. There was one important drawback to Cripps's visit this time: his negotiations would not involve the British viceroy in India.

Indian hopes were dampened by the fact that Cripps was on a strict timetable; he was to make his proposals and then leave. Cripps promised India full dominion status as soon as World War II was over. As a dominion, India would still be a member of the British Commonwealth but would be self-governing. He also stated that India had the right to separate from the Commonwealth of the British Empire. But his statement included one additional provision that would prove disastrous for Indian nationalism. That statement guaranteed any independent community or state within India the right to choose its own form of government. For example, if India's Muslims did not want to be part of a new Indian nation, they could form their own separate country. For the time being, until such sweeping changes took place, the viceroy would hold absolute authority. Several representatives from various Indian political organizations would be invited to join the viceroy's cabinet, but would hold no decision-making power.

Nehru and members of the Indian National Congress debated the Cripps offer. Now Nehru had a new worry. If the British suddenly left India, the Japanese might carry out a full-scale invasion and take over the country. Nehru suggested that India organize its own guerrilla army to fight the Japanese if they invaded India. Nehru had believed that nonviolence should be used against British colonialism, but he thought violence would be necessary against foreign invaders. Gandhi disagreed; only nonviolence could save India from "self-extinction."

Although Nehru respected Cripps and wanted to accept his proposal for Indian independence, he still doubted that the British would keep their promises. He would later remember Churchill's words from 1945: "I have not become His Majesty's first minister

> Long experience has taught us that it is dangerous in the interest of truth to suppress opinions and ideas; it has further taught us that it is foolish to imagine that we can do so. It is far easier to meet an evil in the open and defeat it in fair combat in people's minds, than to drive it underground and have no hold on it or proper approach to it. Evil flourishes far more in shadows than in the light of the day.
> —JAWAHARLAL NEHRU

to preside over liquidation of the British Empire." Still, Nehru thought India had little choice but to accept Britain's offer. If the British, in anger, deserted India, that would make the country vulnerable to a Japanese invasion. Nehru worried that India's army would be powerless against the aggressive Japanese armed forces.

Gandhi, however, opposed the British offer. The Mahatma began demanding that India start another civil disobedience campaign. While the debate in Congress about the Cripps offer intensified, Gandhi proposed a new protest. He called it "Quit India." It was a strong message to the British: "Get out of India at once, or else!"

Nehru thought Gandhi's timing was off. "Nonviolent noncooperation" at this time could endanger not only British rule; it could lead to conquest by Japan. Great Britain was at war, and the Japanese had invaded throughout Asia. This was not the time to protest. When Nehru brought his concerns to Gandhi, the Mahatma told him that to discontinue the struggle against Britain would mean that other countries would remain enslaved. The British might again use harsh penalties against Indian troublemakers. When Congress voted, Gandhi's proposal won.

On August 7, 1942, Congress launched its Quit India campaign. In its resolution the Congress stated, "In making the proposal for the withdrawal of British rule from India, the Congress has no desire whatsoever to embarrass Great Britain or the Allied powers in their prosecution of the war, or in any way to encourage aggression on India. . . ." The resolution closed with a warning that the demand for British withdrawal would be backed up by satyagraha demonstrations led by the Mahatma. India would use all its "nonviolent strength" to achieve this end. Two days later, Gandhi, Nehru, and all the members of the Congress Working Committee were arrested. They were taken to Ahmednagar Fort, a prison located in a remote area of the Bombay Province. This was Nehru's longest prison term. He was behind bars for more than three years. These years, however, were not a complete loss for Nehru. He

Appointed prime minister of an interim government, Nehru listens to tribal leaders during a tour of India's North-West Frontier Provinces in 1946. The British, finally resigned to the inevitability of Indian independence, tried to devise a formula for a transfer of power acceptable to both Hindus and Muslims.

75

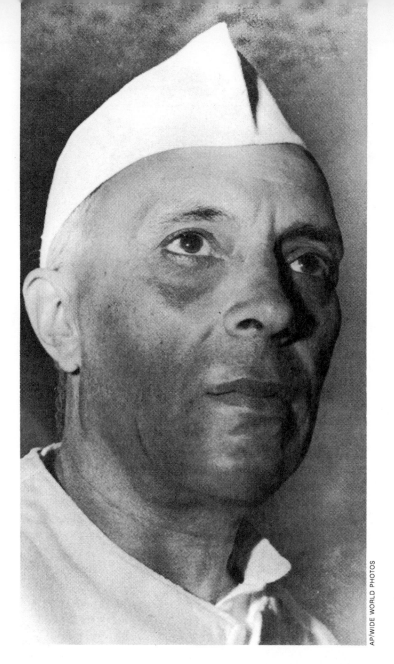

Nehru hoped that India would not be divided. However as it became apparent that Britain would be leaving the country, violence between Hindus and Muslims grew more intense. On a single day in August 1946, more than 6,000 people died during fierce riots in Calcutta.

spent much time in spirited discussions with important colleagues such as A. K. Azad, a Muslim nationalist and member of Congress. Azad had been a supporter of satyagraha and the Quit India resolution. Another was the Hindu antisocialist Sardar Vallabhbhai Patel, who would become deputy prime minister of a free India and who began as Nehru's political rival in the Congress in the 1920s. Nehru had worked closely with both men. In jail, the three leaders argued concerning their differing visions of India's future.

The arrest of India's leaders set off an angry explosion in India. People marched through the streets of Bombay, Delhi, and Madras shouting nationalist songs. They demanded the release of their leaders. Revolt was in the air. The British tightened their controls. First they outlawed the Indian National Congress, then they carried out massive arrests. Once again, violence erupted in the streets, and many lives were lost.

To add to India's problems, the crops failed and a terrible famine struck, leaving many people starving and homeless. In Bengal, more than 1.5 million people starved to death. From his prison cell, Nehru described the horror: "Famine came . . . horrible beyond words. Men and women and little children . . . dropped down dead before the palaces of Calcutta . . . their corpses covered the roads and fields of [Bengal's] rural areas." India's problems worsened each day. Indian soldiers and sailors went on strike and refused to fight for Britain. The British colonial administration lost control of the Royal Indian Navy. India was on a rampage, and the British could no longer govern the country.

The spectacle of what is called religion, or at any rate organized religion, in India and elsewhere, has filled us with horror, and I have frequently condemned it and wished to make a clean sweep of it.
—JAWAHARLAL NEHRU

AP/WIDE WORLD PHOTOS

Nehru and Jinnah meet in London in December 1946. The leader of the Muslim League continued to press for the creation of Pakistan as a separate state and urged Nehru to accept the notion of "partition" to avoid an outright civil war.

77

Lord Mountbatten, the last viceroy of the British *raj* (rule) in India. Mountbatten was sympathetic to Indian nationalism, and was instrumental in forging the settlement that established an independent India and the new nation of Pakistan.

From 1942 to 1945, while the Hindu leaders of the Indian National Congress were in jail, India remained in a state of confusion. The country lacked leadership. During this time Jinnah, the Muslim leader, had a chance to exploit the crisis to his advantage. For many years Jinnah had dreamed of creating a separate country for Muslims, 2 million of whom belonged to the Muslim League. He planned to call the new country Pakistan, or Land of the Pure. Of course, Jinnah also planned to be the leader of Pakistan.

Jinnah campaigned vigorously throughout India to rally Muslim support for a separate Muslim country. He knew that when it was again time to negotiate with the British, the Muslim League would be in an excellent position to argue for the creation of Pakistan. Nehru denounced the Muslim League as taking a position that could "only be understood in terms of the Middle Ages."

During Jinnah's campaign, conditions in India worsened, and the British feared a civil war. Knowing that they could not support a war within the colony, the British decided it was time to cut ties with India. Parliament immediately sent a new negotiating committee to the colony to prepare for withdrawal and to transfer governmental power to India. Much to Prime Minister Churchill's disappointment, Gandhi did not die in prison, despite his extremely frail health, brought about by age and his many hunger strikes. Lord Archibald Wavell, who was appointed viceroy in 1943, obtained permission to release the Mahatma in May 1944.

One plan for a separate Muslim state had already been brought to Gandhi's attention. It called for a border that carefully avoided those areas where the Hindu population was in the majority within Bengal and Punjab, both provinces with an overall Muslim majority. This plan, however, would deprive Pakistan of considerable land and resources. Gandhi offered to meet with Jinnah the summer following his release at the Muslim leader's house in Bombay. The Mahatma's intention was not so much to es-

Gandhi and Nehru in 1946. Nehru served as the chief negotiator for the Indian National Congress during talks with Lord Mountbatten on the transfer of power. Although Nehru and the Congress voted reluctantly for partition, Gandhi opposed the decision.

tablish better relations between Jinnah and the Congress as to expose the impracticalities of Jinnah's demand for a separate Muslim homeland.

On June 25, 1945, the first negotiating conference occurred in Simla, located in a beautiful vacation area high in the Himalayan mountains. Nehru had been released from prison 10 days before these negotiations were to begin. The political situation he found was strange and uncertain. But there was no time to recover from his imprisonment, as he was quickly swept up in the new political whirlwind. This time no one doubted that Britain fully intended to give India its freedom. Negotiations began without incident, and it seemed they would proceed smoothly. Almost everyone hoped that India would remain undivided. Then, suddenly, Jinnah stood up and made a threatening statement. He said, "I would never trust a Hindu dictatorship! I demand a separate country for Muslims." Then he furiously stormed out of the meeting and postponed future negotiations.

Jinnah returned to league headquarters and

Nehru (center foreground) and Gandhi (reclining) seated on a platform at a session of the interim government in 1946. The two leaders tried in vain to stop the sectarian strife, with Gandhi even journeying to the areas where the bloodshed had been especially bad. Still, tens of thousands of Indians continued to perish.

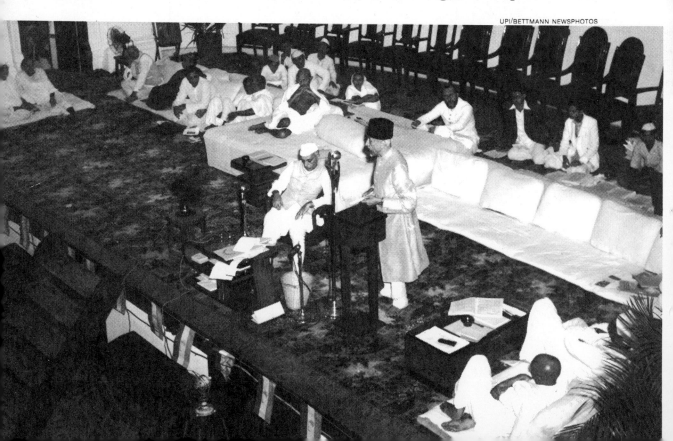

launched a new campaign to rally Muslims. He called for a Muslim Direct Action Day. It was another war cry to his people. Once more, a wave of madness swept India, bringing street violence that continued until August 1947. Muslim gangs fought Hindus in the streets. There was looting and killing. Millions of Indians migrated in an attempt to escape the unrest. Hindu temples were destroyed. In Bengal and Bihar, Hindus and Muslims savagely murdered one another in what became a vicious holy war. In August 1946 the city of Calcutta became the scene of a Muslim uprising in which 6,000 perished. One British newspaper called the events in Calcutta "The Great Killing." In the Punjab Province the Sikhs joined the fighting. They opposed Muslim separatism and wanted to protect their interests.

In February 1946 sailors of the Royal Indian Navy in Bombay began demonstrations against discriminatory treatment. Tempers boiled over into violence, and some British officers were roughed up. British military forces shot at the demonstrators. Mutiny broke out among Indian sailors on British vessels. The ensuing riots in Bombay took 187 lives. Later, Vallabhbhai Patel denounced the bloodshed, while Nehru said that freedom was near. He complained, however, that his countrymen, it seemed, lacked "the discipline which is essential for a free country."

Although Japan's armies were never able to reach India, World War II had greatly affected India's internal affairs. Not since 1937, for example, had any elections been held. Nehru realized that the general elections in the winter of 1945—46 were a way for the nation to evaluate its own political strength. As for the British, they understood that this was a crucial period. The viceroy, Wavell, had proclaimed that India's independence would become a reality after these elections were held.

Nehru hoped that if the Congress party ran its own Muslim candidates in the elections, it could draw away support from the Muslim League and its separatist program. Nehru's hope was not to be realized. What the elections did, however, was to narrow the field. Now there were only two major parties:

> *Every virtue is inextricably intertwined with vice, every vice has something of good in it. And so good and evil march together. Are they opposites or just different sides of reality? I become introspective in jail, and I see a long procession of strangers calling themselves by my name, rather like me and yet different, with something about them that attracts and something that repels. And this long procession of past selves gradually merges into the present ever-changing self. Which of these innumerable shadowselves is me? Or am I all this multitude?*
> —JAWAHARLAL NEHRU
> writing in 1944

Nehru with Indian flag. India became an independent nation at midnight, August 14, 1947. Earlier that day, the British flag had been lowered at ceremonies that Lord Mountbatten said marked "a parting between friends who have learned to honor and respect one another, even in disagreement."

Jinnah's Muslim League and Nehru's Congress party. Nehru worried that the British wanted to restore the princes to their earlier independent control within India. If this happened, it would prove dangerous for India as a whole, since the princely states accounted for one-fourth of the country's population.

Shortly before Muslim nationalism exploded in widespread unrest, Nehru met with Wavell to begin planning an interim government to bridge the gap while India changed status from a colonial possession to a self-governing nation. Nehru was asked to appoint six cabinet members. Jinnah was asked to name five more but refused. When Nehru asked him to form a coalition, Jinnah again refused. An interim government, consisting only of Nehru's appointees, was announced on September 2, 1946.

Throughout 1946, as the violence flared between Hindus and Muslims, the British realized India was on the brink of civil war. They quickly sent a new viceroy, Lord Louis Mountbatten, to help negotiate the transfer of power. Lord Mountbatten was a masterful diplomat, and Nehru knew that Mountbatten favored Indian nationalism. Nehru respected him and was sure that by working together, somehow problems could be resolved. Mountbatten told Nehru that he wished to be thought of as the viceroy who led "the way to the new India."

Although Nehru, Gandhi, and Mountbatten all wanted India to remain one country, to keep peace and avoid more bloodshed they finally agreed to Jinnah's proposal of a Muslim country called Pakistan. India would be partitioned and boundaries established for the new country. As a result of compromise, Pakistan's boundaries would include the North-West Frontier Provinces and the Sind, both in the northwest, where Muslims were the majority. Pakistan would also include the Muslim districts of the Punjab and Bengal, but the areas with a substantial Hindu population within these two provinces would remain in India.

Finally, on August 14, 1947, India was declared an independent nation. The struggle for freedom was finally over. Great Britain was now India's ally and no longer her enemy. At a solemn dedication ceremony in India's Constituent Assembly, an emotional Jawaharlal Nehru rose to his feet and gave the most famous speech of his career:

Long years ago we made a tryst with destiny, and now the time has come when we shall redeem our pledge, not wholly or in full measure but substantially. At the stroke of the midnight hour, when the world sleeps, India will awaken to life and freedom. A moment comes, which comes but rarely in history, when we step out from the old to the new, when an age ends, and when the soul of the nation, long suppressed, finds utterance. It is fitting that at this solemn moment we take the pledge of dedication to the service of India and her people and to the still larger cause of humanity.

Members of India's interim government in November 1946; Nehru is fifth from the left.

AP/WIDE WORLD PHOTOS

7

Prime Minister Nehru

Jawaharlal Nehru was 57 years old when he became India's first prime minister in August 1947. The years ahead were among the most important of his life. In many ways, they were even more difficult than the previous years spent fighting for India's freedom. The transfer of power from the British government to that of India, the creation of Pakistan, and Nehru's efforts to develop his country were enormous challenges.

In previous years, when India's government had been divided between the imperial cities of Bombay and Calcutta, British authorities had allowed 562 Indian princes to govern their own states. Many of the princely states, as they were known, were located close to, or within, the new boundaries of India and Pakistan. When Britain granted to India control over its own governmental affairs, the princes were given the right to decide which country they wanted to join—India or Pakistan.

With the help of Deputy Prime Minister Vallabhbhai Patel, Nehru persuaded most of the princes who ruled states along the Indian border to give up their thrones and join India. To help persuade them,

We have faced, and are facing, the gravest crisis that any government can have to face, more especially a new government. The consequences of each step that we might take are bound to be far-reaching. The world is watching us also and the world opinion counts. But above all we are watching ourselves and if we fail in our own estimation, who will rescue us?

—JAWAHARLAL NEHRU
writing in September 1947

Nehru in London for a conference in 1949, one of the rare occasions on which he wore Western dress. One of the biggest challenges in his early years as prime minister was to fashion a foreign policy for his country. He favored "nonalignment" and traveled to the United States, Britain, China, the Soviet Union, and elsewhere to state his case.

An Indian religious figure
anoints Nehru's forehead on
the eve of India's independence. When Nehru, aged
57, became the first prime
minister of India he em-
barked on what would be the
rest of his life's work — bringing "backward" India into
the modern age.

UPI/BETTMANN NEWSPHOTOS

Nehru and Patel promised the princes a substantial
yearly allowance for the rest of their lives.

The rulers of the two largest remaining princely
states — Kashmir, Nehru's ancestral home, and Hyderabad — were adamantly against the arrange-
ment. They refused to join. The majority of people
in Kashmir were Muslims, but their ruler was a
Hindu. Jinnah wanted Kashmir to join Pakistan.
To accomplish this, he sent volunteer fighters from
Pakistan to capture Kashmir. With Gandhi's reluc-
tant approval, Nehru ordered Indian troops into
Kashmir to fight Jinnah's men. Nehru's troops were
victorious, and after this brief military confronta-
tion, Nehru claimed most of Kashmir as part of India. Later, Nehru was asked to hold an election so

that the people of Kashmir could decide whether or not to join India, but the prime minister insisted it was too late for a vote. Kashmir was already an Indian state.

In Hyderabad, a region as large as France, located in central India, most people were Hindu, but their ruler was a Muslim. Because of his dislike for Jinnah, Hyderabad's ruler, called the Nizam, a shortened form of Nizam-ul-Mulk, meaning "Regulator of the State," wanted an independent state of his own. So he refused to join either Pakistan or India. Negotiations between India and Hyderabad continued for almost a year. At one point, communists (supporters of revolutionary Marxism) established a stronghold in the eastern part of Hyderabad. Militant Muslims known as Razakars had great influence in this state. At first the allies of the Razakars, the communists soon demanded that these extremists give them arms and manpower. The Razakars began to make raids on villages inside Hyderabad. They also terrorized villages in neighboring states. Hyderabad's ruler could not stop the communists or the Razakars. Nehru thought the invaders were a threat to neighboring Indian states. In 1948, after Nehru sent Indian troops to restore law and order, Hyderabad joined India.

Immediately after the new Indian-Pakistani borders were established, Hindus and Muslims suddenly found themselves surrounded by their religious enemies. No one had had time to prepare for the transition. People were frightened. Muslims from the north of India fled to Pakistan. Hindus and Sikhs from Pakistan fled to India to escape their enemies.

Unfortunately, the governments of India and Pakistan were not yet fully organized. Neither could cope with the problems that the partition had created. They were not prepared to care for the 8 million refugees who crossed the new frontiers. The refugees needed food, shelter, and jobs. There weren't enough police to protect the people who fled from one country to another or to stop the violence and bloodshed that erupted in both countries. As a result, one-half million people were killed or died of

Three hundred and fifty million of his countrymen love him [Nehru], follow him, bless him for his brilliant leadership in their struggle for independence, and some say more because of his character, spirit and sacrifice. Long ago he forsook ease and wealth and security to risk life itself for his country.
—ADLAI E. STEVENSON II
American politician

starvation following the partitioning of India.

In January 1948 the Mahatma, now 78 years old, began another fast to protest the killing and violence among Indians and Pakistanis. Each day of his fast, he prayed that Hindus, Muslims, and Sikhs would stop killing one another. After six days of fasting, the fragile old man was terribly weak. Afraid that the great spiritual father of modern India might soon die, religious leaders from India and Pakistan met and agreed to call a halt to the violence. Gandhi ended his fast. But just a few days later, in what was a tremendous shock to the nation, Mahatma Gandhi, on his way to a prayer meeting, was killed by an assassin's bullet. Gandhi was murdered by a Hindu fanatic who thought the Mahatma had been too sympathetic to the Muslims.

The Mahatma's death stunned India. People all over the world were horrified by this brutal killing of a man who had devoted himself to his country's

Nehru visits with Hindus and Sikhs in June 1947. The partition of the subcontinent along religious lines was followed by a massive bloodbath that subsided only when Gandhi fasted in protest in January 1948.

UPI/BETTMANN NEWSPHOTOS

freedom and who always had resisted violence. Nehru, India's grief-stricken prime minister, delivered the eulogy at Gandhi's funeral. With tears in his eyes, he said, "The light has gone out of our lives and darkness reigns everywhere. . . . Our beloved leader Bapu [father] is dead. No more will we run to him for advice or seek solace from him, and that is a terrible blow, not to me alone, but to millions and millions in this land."

After Gandhi's death, Prime Minister Nehru carried the heavy burden of national leadership alone. Nehru and Patel disputed the role of prime minister, and this quarrel continued until Patel's death in December 1950. Nehru maintained the opinion that "in the type of democratic set-up we have adopted, the prime minister is supposed to play an outstanding role." There were many difficult problems to solve and much work to accomplish. India needed a new constitution and a different form of government. Religious hatred was still rampant throughout the country. India could not produce enough food to feed all its people. Ninety percent of the people were uneducated, poor peasants. And by the rest of the world, India was still seen as a "backward nation."

Several members of the constitutional committee, set up by Nehru in 1947, had studied the Constitution of the United States and Britain's parlia-

Nehru addressing a mournful New Delhi crowd on the day after Mahatma Gandhi's funeral. Gandhi, on his way to a prayer meeting, was shot to death by a Hindu fanatic. "The light has gone out," said Nehru, and India and the world were plunged into great sadness.

Nehru (center) and Acharya Vinoba Bhaves (right, with beard), one of Gandhi's oldest disciples, join in a mass spinning exhibition to commemorate the first anniversary of Gandhi's death. Nehru was frequently quoted as saying that the Mahatma was a greater influence on him in death than in life.

mentary system of government. India's constitution (the lengthiest in the world) reflects the democratic principles of both the United States and Great Britain. This constitution was adopted on January 26, 1950.

Like the U.S. Bill of Rights, India's constitution guarantees individual freedoms and rights considered essential to all human beings. At first, the constitutional committee wanted to change the name of India to "The United States of India," but then decided the name might be confusing.

Nehru wanted India's new constitution to emphasize ideas that encouraged national unity. He wanted to eliminate religious separatism among India's Hindus, Muslims, and Sikhs. Although religious freedom was guaranteed to all people, as it is in the United States, Nehru did not want India's laws to be guided by religious laws or traditions.

Under the Indian constitution, "untouchability" was outlawed. The new constitution overturned the traditions that had kept the untouchables separate, granting the same liberties to all persons, regardless of caste, race, sex, or religion.

Nehru also made sure the Indian constitution addressed the problem of communication. Fifteen major languages and more than 1,000 minor languages and dialects are spoken in India. As a result, Nehru knew that many Indians were separated by a lan-

Nehru inspects a women's defense corps in Kashmir in 1948. India's constitution, drawn up under Nehru's direction, reflected his belief in equal freedoms for all. Women, active in the fight for independence, would thus continue to participate in building the new nation.

guage barrier. If they did not learn a common language, their business, educational, and social opportunities in India, as well as throughout the world, would be extremely limited.

The Indian constitution adopted Hindi and English as the country's official languages. Fifteen major languages spoken in India (including English) were also recognized in the constitution. Children in India would be taught three languages in school. Their regional, or community, language would be taught in primary school. Hindi and English would be taught in the higher grades.

Besides a democratic constitution, another of Nehru's major goals as prime minister was improving the standard of living among India's poor. Nehru never forgot the suffering and poverty he saw when he visited the rural peasants of India as a young man. He knew that India's future depended upon

Nehru exchanging the traditional Indian greeting with members of the Indian delegation to the United Nations in 1949. Under Nehru, India became a major voice for the underdeveloped nations of Asia and Africa at the international peacekeeping organization, founded in 1945.

Nehru with famed physicist Albert Einstein during a visit to Princeton University in 1949. The two shared humanitarian ideals and fond memories of Gandhi. Einstein said of Gandhi, "Generations to come will scarce believe that such a one as he ever in flesh and blood walked upon this earth."

the development of a strong economy.

Nehru's popularity as a national leader was confirmed in 1951 when the Congress party won the parliamentary elections by a large majority. As prime minister, Nehru organized a planning commission to help solve India's economic problems. He wanted India to become a modern nation that could feed its population and manufacture profitable goods to sell to other countries.

Nehru's economic planning committee developed three Five-Year Plans. The first Five-Year Plan (1951–56) was designed to teach peasants modern farming methods. This was difficult because most peasants could not read or write. Also, it was hard for them to make the leap from traditional farming methods to modern agricultural techniques. The second plan (1956–61) increased the amount of money invested in farm production, the development of railroads, and communication systems. Nehru's third plan (1961–65) expanded government ownership of India's new factories and industries. The prime minister believed in economic socialism, a system whereby what is produced or manufactured by a society is owned by the government or community, rather than privately by individuals. Profits are then shared by everyone.

Nehru was convinced that India's greatest wealth was its manpower and a commitment to hard work. He said, "Let us get on with work. Let us produce, but what we are producing is not for individual pockets but for the nation, to raise the standard of the people and the common man. If we do that we shall see India progressing rapidly and many of the problems that face us today will be solved. . . . There is no lack of resources in India . . . no lack of human beings, capable, intelligent and hardworking."

In 1959 a reporter asked Prime Minister Nehru what he thought was the most important development in India in recent years. Nehru answered that it was the improvement of educational opportunities for the Indian people. He believed that lack of

Nehru and Prime Minister Liaquat Ali Khan of Pakistan sign an agreement in 1950, settling disputes over minority populations in their countries. Religious tension and rival claims to power on the subcontinent were at the forefront of frequent Indian-Pakistani disputes.

AP/WIDE WORLD PHOTOS

education, particularly among the poor peasants, was one of India's major problems. Most peasants were illiterate. If they did not learn basic skills, their standard of living would never improve. Under Nehru's leadership, many more Indian children went to school and learned to read and write.

Prime Minister Nehru's policies were widely accepted by the people of India. Like his great teacher Mahatma Gandhi, Jawaharlal Nehru was now given a special title of respect by the people of India. They called him *Pandit*, or Wise One. And wherever he went, people greeted him with a Hindi cheer, *Panditji-Ki-Jail*, meaning "Victory to Pandit Nehru."

Nehru at a press conference in the 1950s. As his popularity at home and abroad increased, Nehru was accorded a special title of respect by the Indian populace: *Pandit*, **or Wise One. Indeed, India's moral stature and influence in world affairs were largely due to Nehru's efforts.**

8

The Last Years

During his first few months in office, Prime Minister Nehru lived in a small house in New Delhi with his daughter Indira and her family. In March 1942 Nehru's daughter Indira had married a journalist named Feroze Gandhi. Feroze had the same last name as the Mahatma but was not related to him. By 1947 Indira, who would become president of the Congress party and, in 1966, prime minister of India, had two young sons, Rajiv and Sanjay. The Gandhis' house was so tiny and crowded that Nehru erected a tent outside the property to give the family more room. The old family mansion, Anand Bhawan, was no longer owned by the Nehrus. Before he died, Jawaharlal's father, Motilal, had changed the name of their family home to *Swaraj Bhawan*, or "House of Freedom," and donated it to the nation as a memorial to India's struggle for independence. Swaraj Bhawan is now a national museum in the city of Allahabad.

By 1948 Prime Minister Nehru had moved into his official residence in the capital of India, New Delhi. It was a huge mansion formerly occupied by the British generals who had commanded India's

> *The basic fact of today is the tremendous pace of change in human life.*
> —JAWAHARLAL NEHRU
> his personal motto

Nehru chose a careful course for such domestic concerns as social reform, agricultural production, and industrial development. In the 1950s, he realized that India's greatest strength — her huge population (then about 450 million) could also be the nation's worst handicap.

Our main stake in world affairs is peace and to see that there is racial equality and that people who are subjugated become free. For the rest we do not seek to interfere and we do not desire other people to interfere in our affairs.
—JAWAHARLAL NEHRU
speaking in March 1949

AP/WIDE WORLD PHOTOS

Nehru and his daughter, Indira, in 1963. Indira had grown up among the Indian nationalists and had her father's devotion to India. In 1966, after many years of political activism at her father's side, she would become India's prime minister.

armed forces. The interior was decorated in grand aristocratic style. There were large, spacious rooms with high ceilings. Reminders of Britain's impact on India's history were everywhere. Large paintings of various British military leaders hung on the walls. India's prime minister did not find himself at all comfortable amidst these relics of the colonial past.

Although Indira had her own family to care for, she spent much time with her father. She knew he depended on her and needed her help. Since Indira's mother had died in 1936, India was without a "first lady." Indira felt it was her duty to serve as her father's official hostess. She not only redecorated the New Delhi mansion, she also planned the meals, supervised the household, and entertained the foreign dignitaries who visited.

Within a short time, Indira and her children moved into the mansion. Indira's husband worked in the city of Lucknow, more than 200 miles away. He visited his wife and sons as often as he could.

Prime Minister Nehru kept a very demanding schedule. Every day he worked from 7:00 A.M. until well after midnight. There were scores of government papers to read and approve, endless decisions to make, and a steady stream of political leaders to see. Sometimes, when he was very tired during the day and needed to relax, he meditated or did the yoga exercises Mahatma Gandhi had taught him.

Unlike the Mahatma, Prime Minister Nehru was not a vegetarian. He ate meat and liked many different kinds of food. He enjoyed European food as well as Indian food. He told the family cook he preferred to drink "coffee with milk in the morning and wcak tca in the afternoon," but sometimes he was so busy he skipped breakfast or lunch.

Prime Minister Nehru speaking to visitors at his official residence in 1960. Every day, for one hour, Nehru held public forums with Indian citizens who had come to him with problems or suggestions or even questions of political theory.

AP/WIDE WORLD PHOTOS

Nehru with Vietnamese Communist leader Ho Chi Minh during a trip to Hanoi in 1954, the year French forces were driven from Vietnam. Nehru also visited Chinese Communist leader Mao Zedong that same year. Both Nehru's journeys and his neutrality toward the West's campaign against communism led to criticism of the prime minister in Europe and the United States.

Whenever he had time, Nehru enjoyed playing with his grandsons, Rajiv and Sanjay. The boys loved to visit their grandfather's animal collection. Since childhood, Nehru had always enjoyed caring for animals. When he was prime minister, he installed a private zoo on his property so he could observe and study the behavior of many different kinds of animals, including lion and tiger cubs. When the cubs grew large, Nehru donated them to a public zoo.

In addition to his duties as prime minister, Nehru was also India's chief foreign minister. Since the day in 1927 when he had first addressed an international conference in Brussels, he took a keen interest in international relations. Now that India was an independent nation, Prime Minister Nehru wanted his country to participate in international affairs. In his political involvements Nehru seldom sided with a particular group that was warring with another; instead, he chose to seek an alternative position whenever possible. This style could be found in the foreign policy principles he established for India. Nehru firmly backed, and helped formulate, the principles of nonaggression and mutual betterment. He advised certain leaders of other nations that had recently gained self-rule to seek non-aligned status in diplomacy. This meant not becoming entangled with, or committed to, another nation's foreign policy. One leader who listened seriously to Nehru was Egypt's President Gamal Abdel Nasser.

The prime minister believed it was important for India to maintain friendly relations with other countries. If India needed economic help, the country could then turn to other nations for assistance. Nehru wanted to keep relations as friendly as possible with all countries — especially China, the Soviet

> *He [Nehru] was not one man but a procession of men. In him you witnessed a national hero, statesman, philosopher, historian, author, educator.*
> —NORMAN COUSINS
> American journalist

Nehru visits a collective farm in the Soviet Union in 1955. The Indian leader was impressed with the Soviet government's success at modernizing a backward nation, and the two countries signed a major trade agreement and enjoyed warm relations for much of Nehru's tenure as prime minister.

Nehru (daughter Indira behind him) and President Nikolai Bulganin of the Soviet Union sign a statement in 1955 calling for a complete ban on nuclear weapons and a substantial reduction in conventional arms. (At far right is Nikita Khrushchev, Soviet premier until 1964.) Nehru was one of the world's first major spokesmen to advocate bringing an end to all nuclear testing.

Union, the United States, France, and Britain.

In one of his speeches to the Indian legislature, Prime Minister Nehru described his view of India in world affairs: "I have no doubt at all that we have to learn a great deal from Europe and America and I think that we should keep our eyes and ears completely open . . . but . . . we should not allow any wind from anywhere to sweep us off our feet. . . . If by any chance we align ourselves definitely with one power group . . . it may do harm to India . . . and to world peace. . . . We seek no domination over any country. We do not wish to interfere in the affairs of any country."

While he was prime minister, Nehru made more than 24 trips to foreign countries to meet other world leaders. It was an exhausting travel schedule. He often napped on airplanes en route from one country to another. Nehru visited the United States in 1949, 1956, and 1961.

Many foreign dignitaries also visited Nehru in New Delhi. These visitors included the Dalai Lama of Tibet (the high priest, whom Nehru's government allowed to take refuge in India when he fled from the Chinese Communists), Nikita Khrushchev and Nikolai Bulganin, the leaders of the Soviet Union, Zhou Enlai, then premier of China, and Gamal Abdel Nasser of Egypt. Among his visitors from the United States were Eleanor Roosevelt, wife of Franklin Roosevelt, the former president, and Jacqueline Kennedy, wife of President John Kennedy, who was cut down by an assassin's bullet in 1963.

Nehru visiting Harrow, his boyhood alma mater, during a trip to England for a Commonwealth conference in 1960. The irony of being cheered in the country whose leaders ordered his imprisonment a generation or two earlier was one of many poignant moments in the Indian leader's life.

Nehru and Kwame Nkrumah, then leader of Ghana, at a Commonwealth conference in London in 1957, the year the African nation gained independence from Britain. Nkrumah, a strong supporter of Nehru's "nonaligned" movement among Third World nations, shows the Indian prime minister a small Ghanaian flag.

Nehru and Chinese Premier Zhou Enlai in Beijing, 1954. Nehru and Zhou established a good rapport, but Zhou later forfeited that trust when the Chinese annexed Tibet in 1959 and when the Chinese Red Army invaded India and seized 16,000 square miles of its territory in 1962.

Although Prime Minister Nehru was respected throughout the world as a great leader and diplomat, the United States did not always approve of his foreign policy. During the 1950s the United States strongly criticized Prime Minister Nehru's policy toward the communist People's Republic of China. Nehru remained neutral toward China when the United States fought the Chinese Communists in Korea. However, relations between China and India became increasingly tense, starting in 1959, and Nehru realized he had misjudged his neighbor. In 1962 the Chinese Red Army invaded India's North-East Frontier Agency (later renamed Arunachal Pradesh). The Indian army was soundly defeated in several battles near the Chinese-Indian border. Nehru was shocked and disappointed to think that the Chinese Communists had lied to him. Zhou Enlai had promised never to attack India. Zhou was a particularly cunning statesman, however, and Nehru realized he had made a serious miscalculation concerning the Chinese Communists. Both Britain and the United States immediately sent military aid to Nehru to help India repel the communist invaders in north India.

The responsibilities of Nehru's office and the heavy work schedule he had imposed on himself began to take their toll. His strikingly handsome face showed signs of strain and weariness. His shoulders, once straight and square, were now slightly hunched. In 1958 the fatigue of so many years at the helm of Indian politics caused Nehru to want to resign from office. He felt his ideas were getting "stale." He wanted to take some time to rest and rethink his ideas. But members of the Indian Parliament and his associates in the Congress party begged him to stay. One of his close friends said, "Panditji, if you leave us we will be orphans." Nehru agreed to continue for another term of office. But during the 1960s Nehru's health began to fail. At a Congress party meeting on January 8, 1964, he suddenly slumped, unconscious, in his chair. He had suffered a major stroke. Indira was at his side and helped carry her father from the room.

The prime minister never regained his health. He

was bedridden for the remainder of his life. He died in a coma on May 27, 1964, at age 74.

Once, while discussing India's and his own future, Nehru was asked how he would like to be remembered when he left this world. He said, ". . . if any people choose to think of me then, I should like them to say: 'This was a man who, with all his mind and heart, loved India and the Indian people. And they, in turn, were indulgent to him and gave him of their love most abundantly and extravagantly.' "

On the day of Prime Minister Nehru's funeral, more than a million people lined the streets of New Delhi to pay tribute to him. They watched and wept as they bade farewell to their beloved national leader. In a solemn procession, Nehru was carried to a place near the Jumna River where his respected teacher, Mahatma Gandhi, had been cremated. Nehru's body was attired in his customary white

Nehru died on May 27, 1964. Here his body is carried on a stretcher to his residence in New Delhi to be placed for public viewing. Following Hindu custom, his body was cremated and his ashes were scattered across the holy Ganges River.

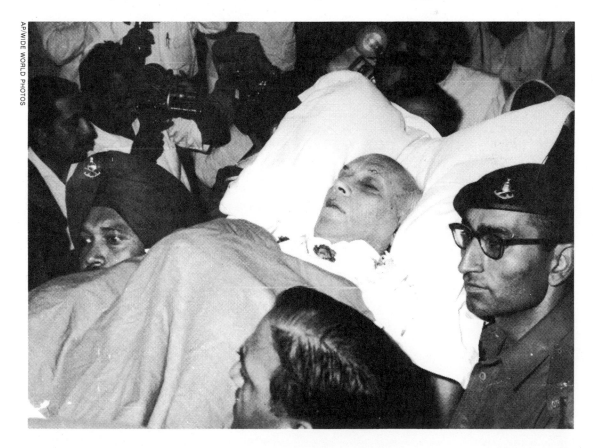

The crowded streets of Calcutta, India. In the early 1970s, 40 percent of all Indians were living on less than 12 cents a day. The slums and general poverty of India's largest city have come to symbolize throughout India and the world the impoverished condition under which most Indians live.

UPI/BETTMANN NEWSPHOTOS

homespun jacket with a red rose in the buttonhole.

In the Hindu tradition, the body was placed on a funeral pyre for cremation. Holy men chanted prayers as Nehru's grandson Sanjay lit the match to ignite the fire. Later, as he had requested before his death, Nehru's ashes were placed in an urn and carried to the sacred Ganges River, where they were scattered in the flowing waters.

Believing that education and democracy were the safeguards of liberty, Nehru was a courageous man who was totally dedicated to the cause of Indian freedom and independence. His political and economic views helped modernize a country that was once called "a backward nation."

Nehru, with his original views on foreign policy, brought independent India into the international community. Although his views often stirred controversy and criticism among both Western and Eastern, communist and noncommunist, governments, he was widely respected as a diplomat. He believed it necessary to guard against fear and religious hatred, which were constant dangers to the stability of India. For the 17 years he was prime minister, Nehru was committed to the goal of world peace. In the 1960s he was the first major world statesman to propose a treaty to ban nuclear weapons testing.

Martin Luther King, Jr., was a great admirer and follower of the principles of nonviolent resistance developed by Gandhi and Nehru. The leader of the black civil rights movement in the United States, who was assassinated in April 1968, said of Nehru, "In all the struggles of mankind to rise to a true state of civilization, the towering figure of Nehru sits unseen but felt at all council tables. He is missed by the world, and because he is so wanted, he is a living force in the tremulous world of today."

Greatness comes from vision, the tolerance of the spirit, compassion and an even temper which is not ruffled by ill fortune or good fortune. It is not through hatred and violence or internal discord that we make real progress. As in the world today, so also in our country, the philosophy of force can no longer pay and our progress must be based on peaceful cooperation and tolerance of each other.
—JAWAHARLAL NEHRU

Nehru with his grandson Rajiv in 1947. Following Prime Minister Indira Gandhi's assassination at the hands of her Sikh bodyguards in 1984, Rajiv succeeded her as India's head of state. As one of "midnight's children" — those born around the time of India's independence — he faced, at age 40, the formidable task of governing the vast nation that had been led by his mother, Indira, and his grandfather, Nehru.

Further Reading

Ali, Tariq. *An Indian Dynasty.* New York: G. P. Putnam's Sons, 1985.

Brecher, Michael. *Nehru: A Political Biography.* Boston: Beacon Press, 1962.

Bush, Catherine. *Mohandas K. Gandhi.* New York: Chelsea House Publishers, 1985.

Butler, Francelia. *Indira Gandhi.* New York: Chelsea House Publishers, 1986.

Crocker, W. R. *Nehru.* New York: Oxford University Press, 1966.

Lamb, Beatrice P. *The Nehrus of India.* New York: Macmillan & Company, 1967.

Mabbett, Ian W. *A Short History of India.* New York: Praeger Publishers, 1970.

Moore, Clark D., and D. Eldridge, eds. *India Yesterday and Today.* New York: Praeger Publishers, 1970.

Moraes, Frank. *Jawaharlal Nehru.* New York: Macmillan & Company, 1956.

Nehru, Jawaharlal. *Jawaharlal Nehru: An Autobiography.* London: The Bodley Head, 1936.

Pandey, B. N. *Nehru.* New York: Stein & Day, 1976.

Traub, James S. *India: The Challenge of Change.* New York: Julian Messner, 1981.

Chronology

Nov. 14, 1889	Born Jawaharlal Nehru in Allahabad, India
1910	Graduates from Cambridge University, England
1912	Passes law examinations at the Inner Temple, London; returns to India
Feb. 1916	Marries Kamala Kaul in Delhi
Nov. 19, 1917	Daughter Indira — who would later serve as prime minister of India — is born
April 13, 1919	British troops massacre nearly 400 Indian peasants at Jallianwalla Bagh garden, Amritsar
1920–21	Nehru devotes himself fully to Gandhi's non-violent resistance movement; tours rural areas extensively to organize peasants
1926–27	Lives in Europe while his wife is receiving treatment for tuberculosis
Dec. 1929	Elected president of the Indian National Congress
Jan. 26, 1930	The Congress declares Independence Day, vowing to seek complete independence from the British Empire
March–April 1930	Gandhi leads his followers on a 241-mile march to protest British monopoly control over the Indian salt industry (the Salt March)
Feb. 6, 1931	Motilal Nehru, Jawaharlal's father, dies at Allahabad
May 1933	Gandhi's three-week fast on behalf of the untouchables leads to a disagreement with Nehru
Feb. 28, 1936	Kamala Nehru dies in Switzerland
Aug. 7, 1942	Congress launches the "Quit India" campaign of civil disobedience, which leads to violent British reprisals
1946–47	Nehru serves as leader of the interim government of India Sectarian violence between Muslims and Hindus claims the lives of thousands
Aug. 15, 1947	India achieves independence, becoming a British dominion Nehru is named India's first prime minister
1947	India is partitioned into two separate nations: India and Pakistan
Jan. 26, 1950	India is proclaimed an independent republic under a new Indian constitution
April 1, 1951	Nehru launches the first of three Five-Year Plans intended to modernize the Indian economy
1956–62	Nehru advocates policy of neutrality and non-alignment in world affairs
Oct. 1962	Chinese Communists invade India and annex border territory after defeating the Indian Army
May 27, 1964	Nehru, age 74, dies at New Delhi

Index

Lila Finck is a freelance writer who specializes in history. A former teacher, she has also written educational training materials for children. She resides with her husband in Melrose Park, Pennsylvania.

John P. Hayes, Ph.D., is a Philadelphia-based freelance author and college professor. He is the author of *James A. Michener: A Biography,* and many other books and articles. Dr. Hayes, his wife, and three children reside in North Hills, Pennsylvania.

Arthur M. Schlesinger, jr., taught history at Harvard for many years and is currently Albert Schweitzer Professor of the Humanities at City University of New York. He is the author of numerous highly praised works in American history and has twice been awarded the Pulitzer Prize. He served in the White House as special assistant to Presidents Kennedy and Johnson.